THE · BUSINESS · SIDE · OF · GENERAL · PRACTICE

 # General Practice Employment Handbook

NORMAN ELLIS

Under Secretary, British Medical Association

FOREWORD BY

JOHN CHISHOLM

Chairman
General Medical Services Committee
British Medical Association

CAROLE LAWRENCE-PARR

Chairman
Association of Managers in General Practice

RADCLIFFE MEDICAL PRESS

Radcliffe Medical Press Ltd
18 Marcham Road, Abingdon, Oxon OX14 1AA, UK

British Library Cataloguing in Publication Data

A catalogue record for this book is available from the British Library.

ISBN 1 85775 234 1

Library of Congress Cataloging-in-Publication Data is available.

Typeset by Advance Typesetting Ltd, Oxfordshire
Printed and bound by Biddles Ltd, Guildford and King's Lynn

 # Contents

Preface

This book draws heavily upon a previous publication, *Employing Staff*, which was published by the British Medical Journal from 1984 to 1997. The move to a new publisher has provided an ideal opportunity to substantially revise the text. The book deals with those problems that are most likely to arise in general practice and it is essential reading because employers have a wide range of legal duties that they should not forget or neglect. Much of this law is complex, and because existing books and articles on this subject are mostly written for the large organization it has been necessary to provide a practical and simplified account that is accessible to the small employer.

Employment law is continually evolving. It is remarkable just how many changes have had to be made to the text since the fifth edition of *Employing Staff* was published in 1994. In particular, the recently enacted Disability Discrimination Act introduces important new rights for disabled employees and imposes substantial new duties on employers. At this stage there is widespread ignorance of the Act. However, it shows every prospect of taking many employers by surprise as has health and safety legislation during the past two decades. Other significant legal changes include the removal of the 16 hour and eight hour thresholds for employment rights and the greatly expanded maternity rights. Because a very high proportion of practice staff are part-timers, the greatly increased statutory employment rights of part-timers has important consequences for practices.

Entirely new chapters are included on:

- fixed term contracts
- employed or self-employed?
- GP registrar contracts
- disability discrimination
- NHS pensions for practice staff.

At the time of writing an industrial tribunal has held that rules which deny over-65s the right to claim unfair dismissal or redundancy breach European sex equality law. The tribunal decided that the rules were discriminatory because more men than women want to work after 65. Although tribunal rulings do not set a precedent, if the case is subsequently upheld on appeal it will open up the way for both men and women over age 65 to claim employment protection rights.

A further area where important changes to employment protection law seem likely is the minimum length of service required to acquire protection against unfair dismissal. It is currently expected that the Government will soon announce a reduction in this threshold from two to one year.

Only a general guide to the provisions of existing legislation is provided in the chapters that follow. No attempt has been made to offer a definitive statement of the law.

NORMAN ELLIS
April 1998

Foreword

The fact that this book's forerunner *Employing Staff* reached its fifth edition and that over 16 000 copies were sold to GPs and their practice managers speaks for itself. This new book not only updates its forerunner but also includes several new chapters. *Employing Staff* was the essential guide to this important and complex subject over many years.

There is a large and ever growing body of employment law which has created a plethora of rights for employees and obligations for employers. Employers breach them at their peril. It is well known that ignorance of the law is no defence against its breach and an employer who is found at fault by an industrial tribunal may have to pay up to a six figure compensatory sum.

The basic principles of employment law are brought together and laid out clearly in this important, reliable and readable book which has been written specifically for small businesses. Although it is written very much with general practice in mind, other professions both within and outside the health service could well find it useful.

A final word of advice. When you obtain a copy do keep it close to hand. It is an essential point of reference when employment and personnel problems occur.

JOHN CHISHOLM
Chairman
General Medical Services Committee
British Medical Association

CAROLE LAWRENCE-PARR
Chairman
Association of Managers
in General Practice
April 1998

1 Recruiting staff

When a vacancy occurs • Profile of the person you need • Finding suitable applicants • Application forms • Selecting the best candidate • The interview • After the interview • Job references • Preventing illegal employment • Specimen job description

Where to obtain advice and assistance

BMA members should contact their local BMA office. The Association of Managers in General Practice (AMGP), the Association of Medical Secretaries, Practice Managers, Administrators and Receptionists (AMSPAR) and the Royal College of Nursing should be able to advise on appropriate job descriptions. (*See* Appendices A and B for addresses.)

Good recruitment and selection procedures can improve the running of a practice – for example, by reducing staff turnover. If you choose the right staff they are likely to stay with you and give good and loyal service. If you pick the wrong people they will leave voluntarily when they find more suitable employment or leave involuntarily when you decide they are not suited to the job. Alternatively, you may even unwittingly choose to put up with unsatisfactory or indifferent standards of work.

Unlike large organizations, practices cannot be expected to devote sizeable resources to recruiting and training new staff. But they experience more acute difficulties than the large organization if the staff they recruit prove to be unsatisfactory. Strong personal ties can develop among a small group of staff and any disciplinary action (which may ultimately lead to dismissal) is often more difficult to take. It is only too common to find practices tolerating poor levels of performance from staff simply because they cannot face the unpleasant and difficult task of correcting the problem.

Although the time spent on recruiting and training new staff may seem costly, it is often less costly in the long run than the resources that may be wasted when staff prove to be ill suited to their work. To neglect these matters almost always stores up trouble for the future.

Too often when a practice is faced with staffing difficulties (which may even involve a threat of legal action) the roots of these lie in a failure to recruit the right staff in the first instance and to provide them with the training they require. These shortcomings may be compounded by an innate reluctance to manage. Early difficulties are left uncorrected and unsatisfactory performance and working habits are allowed to persist and are thus tolerated by all concerned. A failure to act in these circumstances is often interpreted (quite understandably) as evidence of tolerance of indifferent standards of performance and unsatisfactory working practices.

When a vacancy occurs

When you have a vacancy it is essential to consider whether it really needs to be filled and, if so, whether the content of the job has changed. (Have there been any changes in work pattern, technology – for example, computerization – or organization since it was last filled?) You should also consider whether there are likely to be future changes in the job which require additional or different skills. A good way of assuring yourself that the job has been thoroughly reviewed is to prepare a 'job description'.

It may seem pedantic to write a detailed description. Is it not sufficient simply to give the job an accurate title? Unfortunately there is no easy way of avoiding the task of preparing a job description if you wish to put relations with staff on a sound footing.

The job description should describe the tasks and responsibilities of the job:

- *main purpose of the job* – try to summarize this as briefly as possible (if you cannot identify a main purpose the job may need to be reviewed)
- *main tasks* – try to use active verbs, such as 'filing', 'answering' and 'helping', rather than less precise terms, such as 'deals with', 'in charge of'
- *scope* – although the 'main tasks' may describe what has to be done, they may not always indicate the job's scope or importance. Under this heading you may need to emphasize the degree of accuracy or precision needed and the number of people supervised.

The length and detail of your job description will vary according to the job. But it is best to aim at providing a clear and simple description. (See Appendix on p. 11 for a specimen job description.)

The job description is important because it tells you what kind of person is needed for the job, enabling you to build a profile of the person you would like to see in the post.

Profile of the person you need

The profile is prepared by devising a list of headings under which you can classify the attributes of the ideal candidate for your vacancy. You may prefer to draft your own headings; those in Table 1.1 merely illustrate how this might be done.

- *Impact on other people* – physical appearance, speech and manner.
- *Qualifications and experience* – education, qualifications, previous work experience. Simple and obvious matters to be considered might include

Table 1.1: Specimen profile of the person to be employed as a receptionist

Necessary	Desirable
Impact on other people	
Acceptable bearing and speech	Pleasant manner, bearing and speech
Qualifications and experience	
Ability to type, to operate PABX telephone equipment, to carry out receptionist and general office work	RSA II typing; previous experience of receptionist work; previous experience of computer technology
Innate abilities	
Ready grasp of a point	Can assess priorities and make decisions quickly
Motivation	
Personal identification with the work of the practice. Interest in maintaining good relations with patients and the efficient running of the practice	Able to work flexibly in an emergency and to do overtime during holiday absences and (at short notice) sickness absences of other staff
Adjustment	
Steady, self-reliant, good at maintaining a pleasant and reassuring relationship with patients and friendly relationship with colleagues at all levels	Able to cope with stress and pressure from both patients and doctors
Health record	
Good. In particular, there should be no previous record of illness that might lead to an abuse of drugs	

typing and audio or shorthand skills, ability to use a word processor and, not least, to be able to write legibly.

- *Ability to learn* – speed of comprehension; ability to learn new skills.
- *Commitment* – what personal goals do the candidates set? Do they pursue these with consistency and determination? How successful have they been in achieving them?
- *Personality* – emotional stability; capacity to work under pressure and to deal with stress. Are they likely to get on with other staff, the doctors and the patients? Another factor that employers in the health sector need to be aware of is its tendency to attract applicants who have a preoccupation with illness (particularly their own ailments).
- *Health record* – in general you should be looking for a good health record. A small practice inevitably finds it more difficult to cope with frequent or long absences. (In particular you will need to be cautious about any previous psychiatric illness that might lead to drug abuse.)

The characteristics identified as necessary from an analysis of your job description should then be entered against the appropriate heading. It is often helpful to enter two levels, indicating what you would be looking for in the ideal candidate and what you regard as a minimum acceptable level. In addition, you should list any personal characteristics or circumstances which would definitely be unacceptable; for example, you would not wish to employ anyone who had an abrasive manner.

How much detail is included in the profile will depend on the job, but not always on the level of the post; for example, a junior post can have important requirements under the heading 'impact on other people'.

If the personnel profile is used as a basis for your interviews it will remind you to be both realistic and systematic. But it must be remembered that there is nothing precise or scientific about a selection procedure. By being systematic you will help to reduce the margin of error. Ultimately you must decide which of the candidates is best suited to fill the job. If after completing the interviews you think that no candidate is suitable do not hesitate to defer an appointment.

Finding suitable applicants

Having written the job description and the personnel profile, you now need to consider the best way of reaching the 'target group' of potential candidates. One method that is often used by practices is word of mouth, sometimes from introductions made by staff or patients. This has obvious attractions: it costs nothing and it helps you to recruit those people from the immediate locality who may have ties of friendship or family with your present staff and the practice. But it may have the disadvantage of perpetuating the existing composition of your staff and it might even lead to allegations of unlawful discrimination. There is also the hidden danger of relaxing your critical faculties and subsequently departing from your carefully prepared personnel profile. It is far too easy to be drawn into appointing someone about whom you feel reassured simply because they have been personally recommended, without having evaluated them against your selection criteria. If this happens and your new employee is subsequently found to be unsatisfactory the already testing business of dismissal is compounded by family or personal ties with other staff.

Many practices have to recruit staff from the area in which their surgeries are located. Sometimes they recruit staff from among their patients. The problems of confidentiality are obvious enough, and at times it may be friends and relatives who pose the greatest potential threat to confidentiality. It is sufficient to emphasize this problem and you should ensure that all staff, particularly new staff, are aware of the importance of maintaining absolute confidentiality and that any breach of confidentiality will be treated as a serious disciplinary matter.

Local schools, colleges and career services can provide candidates who may be suited for your post but if you recruit from these sources you will need to pay extra attention to your arrangements for training new staff. The local newspaper is often the most consistently reliable method of finding candidates, though it can be costly.

Application forms

You may choose between using a standard application form, asking for letters of application or simply taking down information over the phone or at the interview. The advantage of a form is that it is easier to compare like with like, thus helping with the initial sifting of candidates. You, not the candidates, determine what information is included. The standard of completion may be a guide to the candidate's suitability, particularly if clerical skills are important to the job. But application forms do lengthen the selection process and add to administrative costs.

You may wish to include on the application form a statement to the effect that employment in NHS general practice is exempted from the Rehabilitation of Offenders Act 1974 and therefore no applicant is entitled to withhold any information about previous criminal convictions which would otherwise be regarded as 'spent'. The form should also include a section where applicants are asked to give details of any convictions.

Selecting the best candidate

For most vacancies you may want to receive written applications in advance of the interview and to arrange a simple practical test. (It is common practice to test typing skills.)

The partners and the practice manager will need to decide who should be on the interviewing panel. The practice manager usually has an important role in the selection procedure. In some practices the manager carries out a preliminary sift of applications by a first interview, reducing a large number of candidates to a final shortlist. These shortlisted candidates are then asked back for a second interview with both the manager and one or more partners. It is crucial for the practice manager to participate in the final decision. The likelihood of the new employee settling successfully into your practice depends to a great extent on the person who supervises the work and is responsible for seeing that the new recruit is properly trained and made to feel welcome. If your manager has helped to select the new employee, they will naturally feel more committed to the employee. It is also advisable for the candidate to meet the rest of the staff before a decision is made.

References can be helpful but these should be used with care. They are often most useful for checking factual information such as details of previous jobs (length of service, absenteeism, timekeeping etc.). It is particularly important to check on the applicant's previous record of absenteeism and sickness. If you want an opinion on suitability for a specific job, a brief outline of the duties should be sent to the referee and a subsequent telephone conversation may be helpful. (See the section on p. 8 on getting and giving references.)

The interview

Although most jobs are still filled by interview, doubts are sometimes expressed about this method of selection. Despite its limitations, it is widely used and practices will undoubtedly wish to use it to select their staff.

For your interviews to be effective you need to do some careful preparation and they will need to be conducted in an orderly and thorough manner. The interview need not be an over-formal or elaborate exercise.

Three other points should be remembered at the outset. First, you should prepare a checklist of the points to be raised. Second, you may inadvertently enter into contractual obligations (albeit verbal) either in reply to an unexpected question or merely in your attempts to reassure the candidate. Do leave an escape route by emphasizing that the employment contract will be in writing and that it will cover all relevant matters. Third, throughout the interviews you should ensure that none of your questions or answers can be interpreted as discriminatory on grounds of race, colour, nationality (including citizenship) or ethnic or national origins. It is also unlawful for employers to discriminate on grounds of sex, against married persons or against disabled persons. No candidate should be asked questions which are not equally relevant and meaningful to both female and male candidates. Discrimination is prohibited in recruitment and in relation to existing employees.

Your preparation should include the following:

- compare the personnel profile with what you already know about the candidate. Are there any areas of experience or qualifications, for instance, which will need to be explored or clarified? For example, you may decide to test typing and audio skills, and assess computer literacy
- plan your questions. These should probe the candidate's knowledge, ability and attitudes. Some questions should be aimed at a more general assessment of the candidate's personality and wider interests. The health record will need to be discussed and you may wish to seek the candidate's agreement to approach their GP. Ease of travel to work can be important, together with flexibility in approach to working hours. Few practices can work with a rigid attitude to stopping at a fixed time when the bell goes. Finally, the candidate's motives for changing jobs and/or seeking employment are relevant
- if there is more than one interviewer allocate the subjects to be covered
- provide an opportunity for the candidate to ask questions and anticipate the information needed to answer the most likely ones
- be organized, allow enough time, avoid interruptions and have someone available to show candidates to the cloakroom, waiting room etc.

Poor interviews are usually caused by the interviewer being unprepared and unaware of how demanding interviewing can be. In these circumstances the interviewer may talk more than the interviewee and ask leading questions to which the answers are far too obvious. In addition, important aspects of the candidate's previous experience, qualifications, views and attitudes may be left unexplored, so that a proper comparison of candidates cannot be made.

It is useful to have shown the candidate the job description beforehand and to have a copy of your employment contract to hand during the interview. Do ask candidates if they have any questions about the job description. Do not hesitate to mention any demanding and important aspects of the job. It is far better for candidates to learn at this stage than later about any aspect of the job they may not like. It is also advisable to show candidates around the surgery, letting them see what work has to be done, before asking them to commit themselves to the job.

After the interview

After each interview is completed write up notes on your impressions, recording any points strongly for or against the candidate. This will help you to make your final decision, particularly if others participate in the discussion. These notes will also help you to monitor the effectiveness and fairness of your procedures. Your reasons for appointing or not appointing a particular candidate may be important in case you are challenged – for example, under the sex, race or disability discrimination legislation. (It may be worth retaining your notes to refer to if a further vacancy occurs.)

When you have taken your decision inform all the applicants of the outcome. (It cannot be emphasized too often that if you have doubts about the suitability of your preferred candidate do not hesitate to defer the appointment and seek new candidates.) Your letter offering the job should say the date on which employment starts and cover the main headings of the contract. It should also refer to the employment contract which will be issued after the employee has started work.

Job references

Obtaining a reference from a previous employer is normal practice in any recruitment process. However, many employers harbour serious reservations about how much weight should be given to a reference, particularly if it has been provided by someone who is not personally known to them.

The giving and receiving of job references has always been seen as a grey area of the law. Many employers regard the subject as a legal minefield, believing that by providing the least possible information they can safeguard themselves and their organization against the risk of unforeseen and adverse repercussions.

Because references are often written in sparse and defensive terms, employers – who inevitably both send and receive them – only make very limited and cautious use of them.

The Advisory, Conciliation and Arbitration Service (ACAS) acknowledges this problem and suggests that references are probably most useful for checking a limited range of factual information such as job title, length of service and attendance record, which can be easily obtained by asking specific questions or using a standard form. ACAS goes on to suggest that if employers want an opinion about an applicant's suitability for a specific job, the referee should be provided with a brief outline of duties and a telephone discussion may be helpful.

In recent years some important legal cases have helped to reduce the uncertainties surrounding job references. Inevitably most of these cases have been brought by aggrieved employees whose job and career prospects have been critically affected by a previous employer's reference or by a refusal to supply one at all. An unfavourable reference can permanently damage an individual's future career, whereas an over-favourable one can seriously misinform a prospective employer.

Conditional offers

It is normal practice to make a job offer conditional upon receiving satisfactory references from a previous or present employer. If this approach is followed the contract does not come into existence until this condition is met. Thus, if an offer of employment is made expressly conditional on the receipt of satisfactory references and this requirement is not met, the employer may either withdraw the job offer or even fairly dismiss an employee who has already started work.

Prior consent

References should not be requested without having obtained the prior consent of the prospective employee. A prospective employer should be very wary of open references which candidates occasionally bring with them to the interview. These are usually regarded as having little, if any, credibility. The same caution should be applied when candidates provide the names of references who would appear to be personal friends or acquaintances.

Accurate references

It is perhaps surprising that employers are not legally obliged to provide a reference for present or former employees unless their employee's employment contract requires that this should be done. However, it is unusual for an employer to refuse to do so.

Although there is no legal duty as such to provide an employment reference, an employer who does so is obliged to exercise reasonable care and skill in its preparation. Inaccurate references, whether they are favourable or unfavourable, deliberately or unintentionally misleading, can have serious legal consequences.

First, an employee who suffers a loss due to an inaccurate reference may sue for damages on grounds of defamation of character or malicious falsehood. However, the burden of proof is such that it can be very difficult to prove malice. The loss suffered for which damages may be awarded can result from either being unable to gain satisfactory employment or being dismissed because of the unsatisfactory reference.

A second course of action open to an employee is to sue for damages caused by negligence. Because an employer owes a duty of care to the employee when preparing a reference, they should therefore ensure it is both accurate and honest.

Asking for a reference

Basic information to be requested from a previous employer:

- position or job title
- length of service
- competence in the job
- honesty
- timekeeping
- reason for leaving
- any other relevant information such as the employee's sickness or absence record.

However, when you are asked to give a reference for a former employee you may prefer to decline to provide any or all of this information. There is no obligation to be consistent in these matters – you may seek more information than you are prepared to provide yourself.

Finally, although the courts have determined that a former employer also owes a duty of care to a subsequent employer to prepare an accurate and honest reference, many employers continue to include in their references precautionary disclaimers for any omissions or inaccuracies.

Preventing illegal employment

Although it has been a criminal offence since 27 January 1997 to employ anyone contrary to immigration controls, you are not required to check the employment status of anyone employed prior to that date.

A potential employee must not be prohibited from working in the UK. Any employer who illegally employs someone who is not permitted to work can face criminal charges with a maximum penalty of £5000.

To avoid possible difficulties it may be advisable to require a potential employee to produce a document issued by either a previous employer, the Inland Revenue or the Benefits Agency, which clearly shows that they are entitled to work in the UK, and to retain the document or a copy of it. Other documents that may be requested for this purpose include passports and birth certificates.

When undertaking this 'validation' exercise, employers must not discriminate on grounds of race, nationality, colour or ethnic origin. Therefore, all applicants should be treated equally throughout the recruitment process and verification documents should be requested from all potential employees. However, to reduce the administrative burden many employers only apply this verification test to someone finally selected to fill a vacancy, making the job offer conditional upon satisfying UK employment and immigration regulations.

The Home Office has produced a guidance note and has a telephone helpline: 0181 649 7878.

Appendix: Specimen job description

JOB TITLE: RECEPTIONIST

Main purpose of job is to ensure that:

- inquiries from patients are efficiently and courteously handled
- the filing, record keeping and distribution of documents are undertaken efficiently and promptly
- the surgery premises are kept tidy.

Main tasks:

- opening the premises and checking heating and ventilation
- restoring telephone services

- distributing patients' records to the doctors for their surgeries and ensuring that the records of any patients without appointments are available to the doctor when the patient is seen
- setting out letters, new prescriptions and repeat prescriptions for checking by the doctor before collection
- receiving and routeing patients on arrival
- answering general inquiries, explaining surgery procedures, making new and follow-up appointments and receiving requests for repeat prescriptions
- filing and extracting records and any documents relating to these including:
  - filing records of new patients received from the family practitioner committee
  - extracting records of withdrawals from list to send to family practitioner committee
- receiving and recording requests for home visits
- ensuring that an adequate supply of stationery is available in the consulting rooms and the reception area
- receiving messages for nurses and health visitors
- ventilating and tidying waiting room after surgery
- ensuring that the reception area is left tidy and ready for use by incoming colleagues, and that they are provided with information about any unresolved or urgent matters.

2   Looking after your new employee

Why induction matters • When should induction start? • What kind of training is needed? • Confidentiality • Who needs induction? • Who does the induction? • Changes in the GP's terms of service • Continuing education

---

Where to obtain advice and assistance

The Association of Managers in General Practice, the Association of Medical Secretaries, Practice Managers, Administrators and Receptionists, GP Forum, Radcliffe Medical Press and the Royal College of Nursing provide a wide range of training and continuing education courses. (*See* Appendix B for addresses.)

If you have expended effort on recruiting good staff it would be pointless to dissipate this by failing to help them to become accustomed to your practice and to do their jobs satisfactorily. It may seem self-evident that any new employee should be properly trained and introduced into the practice, but it is surprising how often employers neglect or forget this essential task. The staff are a vital asset to the practice and you owe it to them and to yourself to ensure that they are able to contribute to the best of their abilities. If you fail to provide adequate induction and training you may leave yourself seriously at risk if you ever need to take disciplinary action. The term 'induction' may be unfamiliar to you and you may reasonably assume that it is yet another example of technical jargon intruding into the English language, but its use may be justified because it encapsulates the specific task that any employer should undertake.

Why induction matters

You need to help your new employee to settle into the practice as quickly as possible. This means that they should be helped to get to know colleagues and the partners, to become familiar with the surgery premises and to know the wider contacts that will be an important part of the job (for example other practices, the local health authority, local hospitals and the social services department). Above all, they will need to be helped in getting to grips with the job. Of course, a lot of this knowledge may be 'picked up' gradually without any formal induction programme. But there are good reasons for ensuring that this wide range of information is acquired in a planned and systematic way.

When someone starts a new job there is usually some anxiety about some aspects of it. The new recruit is faced with new colleagues, a new boss, new tasks and a new environment. Helping them to settle in is not just a matter of courtesy and consideration, it also contributes to the smooth running of the practice. Induction is just as important in a small organization as it is for those large organizations that run formal training courses, and doing it properly need not be costly in time or resources. But to neglect or forget it may prove very costly indeed.

Until your new employee has settled down they are unlikely to be fully responsive to the demands of the job. There is always an initial (and often steep) learning curve to be surmounted and until this is achieved the new recruit is unlikely to respond quickly and effectively to the demands of the job. The time lag before a satisfactory performance is achieved is likely to be increased if there is no induction programme. Your instructions may be misunderstood or forgotten, and important procedures neglected. The new employee's initial enthusiasm for the job may soon wane and they may become disenchanted and even resign. If discontented, the new employee is unlikely to be effective and may even cause friction in the practice. A new and inexperienced colleague may even have an unsettling influence (albeit unintended) on other staff, so there is a strong case for speeding up integration into the practice. If you get the induction programme right you can avoid these problems. You will have helped your new recruit to settle in and to develop a loyalty and commitment to your practice. Of course, if they become disenchanted and subsequently leave, all the time and effort that you have spent on recruitment has been wasted.

When should induction start?

In fact, induction actually begins when recruiting the new employee. Any applicant should learn something about general practice and how the surgery runs. A new employee is likely to form some first impressions of prospective colleagues (*see* Chapter 1). After someone has been selected for the post it may be helpful to invite them to meet colleagues informally before accepting the job. In a small, tight-knit unit it is crucial that staff should be compatible and that conflicts of personality do not occur.

The next stage is to ensure that there is a welcome on the first day. Although you may be busy and preoccupied with the normal daily pressures of the surgery, a special effort should be made to give full attention to the newcomer. Why not ask the new employee to come later on their first day – for example, after morning surgery has ended – so that you can then give them your undivided attention.

Induction may be spread over several days or even weeks. In a small organization it should not take long. However short the induction programme, it should be comprehensive. Newcomers can absorb only a limited amount of information at a time, but, on the other hand, the more established they become the more difficult it is to set aside time for induction. It is important to allow time for your new employee to gain confidence in the job. There is likely to be a high and continuous pressure of work from the moment the new recruit arrives until the end of the day. It is unlikely that this pressure of work was experienced in a previous job. It may even lead to an early resignation. Thus, it is important to ensure that they are gradually eased into the new working pattern.

What kind of training is needed?

Induction training is likely to be informal but nevertheless it should follow a plan, which may be written as a checklist to ensure that all stages are covered (*see* Table 2.1).

It is likely that much of the induction training will be undertaken by the practice manager and/or other experienced practice staff. Although the specific tasks may be delegated, one person should take overall responsibility for ensuring that the training is completed. In addition, a partner should take a personal interest in the new employee and ensure that they develop satisfactory working relationships with other doctors. To a new employee, particularly a young person, the doctors themselves can seem

Table 2.1:   An induction checklist

First day at work
- Layout of surgery
  - cloakroom and toilet facilities
  - first aid provision
  - 'mess' arrangements
  - lockers

- The job (refer to job description as appropriate)
  - new entrant's own job
  - supervision arrangements
  - colleagues (including introductions to partners)
  - standards of work expected

Second day at work
- Explaining the conditions of employment (refer to employment contract as appropriate)
  - hours of work
  - lunch and tea breaks
  - periods of notice
  - timekeeping
  - method of paying salary
  - income tax, national insurance and any other deductions
  - holidays
  - sick leave, medical statement and rules, e.g. arrangements for reporting absences
  - pension scheme

Third day at work
- The practice
  - range of services to patients
  - organization of practice
  - relations with other bodies and organizations
  - brief history and outline of future developments

remote and unapproachable. Direct contact between one partner and the new employee helps to break down these barriers and also ensure that the practice's clinical objectives are understood.

During the induction programme a new recruit will need to listen to colleagues explaining their work and how the surgery runs, and to watch the pattern of work. They should be encouraged to ask questions, however basic or simple they may seem. Reference may also be made to the employment contract and job description when explaining how the practice is organized and how the new recruit's job fits in.

Confidentiality

Because confidentiality is so important in general practice, it is necessary to give it special emphasis during the induction process. If you want to be able to discipline staff who breach confidentiality, you must make it a contractual requirement and ensure that it is explained fully to your staff when they are undergoing their induction training and is also continually reinforced through your disciplinary procedures.

Industrial tribunal cases arising from practice staff being dismissed over breaches of confidentiality are not uncommon. Such cases can be won if the practice rules include an explicit confidentiality clause which emphasizes that only the partners can make decisions about releasing patient health information, and if it can be shown that this clause has been reinforced during training. The training should emphasize the practice's procedures in relation to confidentiality and the importance of respect for the patient's right to privacy. The practice should be able to show that any breach of confidentiality is treated as a serious matter, regardless of the sensitivity of the information released. If a breach of confidentiality does occur, you should adhere closely to your disciplinary procedure. A thorough investigation is essential, especially if there is any doubt about the identity of the employee who breached confidentiality.

Who needs induction?

Anyone who is new to your practice (or even someone who is transferred from another job) needs some induction. But there are particular groups of people who may need special help and advice. It is not surprising to find that no induction is provided for an employee who is transferred from another job or is promoted. Often it may not be necessary. But it is never advisable to assume that a highly competent senior receptionist will automatically become an effective practice manager immediately after promotion. Indeed, internal promotions in a small organization may create special difficulties; you should not expect someone easily to assume managerial authority and responsibility over colleagues who were formerly 'equals'. If the promotion is to be successful for all concerned, one partner may need to put aside time regularly to advise and assist the newly promoted manager.

Never assume that someone who was recruited from a similar position in another practice will easily slot into your practice. New staff from other practices may have firm preconceptions about how the job should be done which do not fit in with your own arrangements. They may need retraining to understand and apply the methods and philosophy of your practice.

Certain other groups may need special help. School leavers or young people without any experience of employment may be excited yet nervous about their first job. Indeed, they may need to be helped in a sympathetic but firm way to understand the discipline of working life, in particular punctuality, reliability, courtesy to patients and the need to have a positive attitude to work. Anyone returning to work after a long absence may also find difficulty when readjusting to working life. Special help may also be needed if you employ a disabled person or a member of a minority ethnic group.

Who does the induction?

Although several people may be concerned in the induction programme, it is advisable to identify one person who has overall responsibility for it. In most practices the practice manager will have the main responsibility (and the greatest interest) in ensuring that the new employee settles in and quickly becomes an effective member of staff. If the newcomer is a receptionist or secretary the practice manager or another experienced member of staff is best equipped to provide much of the initial training. They will be most familiar with the newcomer's job and be close at hand to advise and assist. Above all, someone must be given specific responsibility for this task; your new employee should know who to turn to for guidance or reassurance.

How you approach the induction of new employees will clearly depend on the circumstances of the practice and the resources that you can devote to it. Induction need not be an elaborate business, but it should be well thought out, planned ahead and then undertaken with care.

The effort and care your practice commits to the induction of a newcomer should result in a more effective and settled employee. Although it may be self-evident that any employer would want to ensure that a new employee is quickly trained to do the job and encouraged to feel at home in the practice, this task is often neglected. It is too easy to assume that the newcomer will automatically acquire the necessary skills and knowledge for the job and there is no need to make any special arrangements for this learning process.

Changes in the GP's terms of service

The terms of service were amended in 1990 and now require all National Health Service general practitioners to take reasonable care to satisfy themselves that their employees are suitably qualified and competent to undertake the work delegated to them. In particular, they are required to take account of academic and vocational qualifications (where appropriate), and training and experience.

Continuing education

Training does not, of course, end when induction is completed. The ever-increasing demands on general practice today mean that it is essential for staff to be encouraged to update and develop their skills and knowledge. There is a wide range of training and continuing education courses available. Training is not simply a matter of attending and acquiring qualifications. Informal practice meetings can contribute to staff education, particularly if care is taken to ensure that the subject matter relates to the work of the practice. These meetings can be particularly beneficial if they are sufficiently informal to encourage staff to contribute freely to the discussion.

3 The employment contract

A simple precaution • The 'implied terms' of an employment contract • Avoiding litigation by good management • Your legal obligations • Rights of the employee • Remedies available to employees • How to introduce a written contract • Draft contract of employment • Notes on the draft contract

Where to obtain advice and assistance

BMA members should contact their local BMA office. The Association of Managers in General Practice, AMSPAR and the RCN should be able to advise on appropriate job descriptions. Health authorities may also be able to advise on employment contracts.

Some GPs who are employers seem to be unaware of their legal responsibilities. Whenever I meet a group of general practitioners surprisingly I still find that some of them have not yet provided staff with a written statement of main terms and conditions (which I refer to as a written employment contract) even though the law requires that in most circumstances this should be done and health authorities have also insisted that a written contract should be in place. This does not mean that no contract actually exists. A verbal (unwritten) contract exists when an offer of a job is made and accepted. And this contract can last for years on a verbal and unwritten basis, capable of being interpreted and enforced by the courts. But verbal contracts, although superficially attractive for their flexibility and apparent simplicity, may lead to serious problems if differences of opinion arise. This is why successive governments, both Conservative and Labour, have introduced legislation to promote written employment contracts.

Surprisingly, but understandably, the employment relationship is often left undocumented, even though all employees (irrespective of how many hours a week they work) have a right to a written contract of employment, which must be provided within two calendar months. A small employer may have little time to devote to the task of writing down the various details of a contract – for example, sick pay, holidays, pensions and disciplinary and grievance procedures – and it often seems preferable to allow these to evolve 'naturally' as the working relationship develops. A written contract is not only troublesome to prepare but might seem to jeopardize a happy working relationship by introducing into it excessive formality and inflexibility. Because working relations between the practice and its staff are close, the formal written contract is seen as an intrusion, bringing the formality of the law into what are essentially personal relations. This reason is also given to explain away forgetfulness.

But the neglect of the written contract is also surprising. Irrespective of whether it is written or not, a legal contract of employment does exist, and therefore the law already has a major part to play. The value of documentation is simply to state in writing the agreements and understandings that already define relationships between the practice and its staff. There are many other contractual relations – for example, mortgage agreements, car purchase, television rental, bank loans – which no employer would consider entering into without proper documentation spelling out in detail the agreement with the other party. But the employment contract may entail far greater liabilities and costs than even a rental or purchase agreement if it should turn sour. Yet the rights and obligations of this contract are often left to verbal understandings and agreements, which may so easily lead to misunderstandings and disagreements.

A simple precaution

I shall not attempt to describe the plethora of employment law. This would be fruitless; practices have enough to worry about without trying to become expert on such matters. Instead, I advise on a course of action that is simple to follow and which should help to avoid most pitfalls.

First, I would strongly advise anyone who has not already done so to provide *written* contracts of employment. Of course, I would also advise caution before rushing into the surgery with a bundle of contracts. Such a gesture can be so easily misunderstood, creating, rather than avoiding, problems.

Second, if care is taken in preparing the contract it will take full account of existing employment law and clarify many matters where there is uncertainty on both sides. The draft contract, on pp. 30–35, takes full account of existing statute law. It even takes account of health and safety legislation by including a policy statement on health and safety at work. (The Health and Safety at Work Act requires every employer of five or more staff to prepare a *written* statement of their general policy, management and arrangements for health and safety at work.)

Finally, the British Medical Association's local offices can provide specialist advice and help to members and their practice managers on how to provide written contracts to staff. This service has been widely used by members; many have made use of the draft contract they can provide.

The 'implied terms' of an employment contract

No written contract, however detailed, can be completely comprehensive. There will always be some aspects of the employment relationship that inevitably remain undocumented but still form part of the contract. The most important of these are known as the implied terms. Thus, an employment contract usually comprises terms that are both express, i.e. written, and implied, i.e. unwritten.

The implied terms are those that the law assumes to be central to the employer/employee relationship. Indeed, these implied terms are so fundamental to the contract that breach of them is a more common cause of disciplinary action and dismissal than express terms.

Of course, if the employer chooses to codify them, they are no longer implied but express terms. The following implied terms are invariably assumed by the courts to be part of an employment contract:

- the employee should serve the employer faithfully – in any contract of employment it may be presumed that this duty of fidelity applies. For example, 'borrowing from the till' would be regarded as being in breach of this, and restrictive covenants are based on this duty
- the relationship between an employer and employee is based on 'mutual trust and confidence' – this implied duty applies equally to both parties
- an employee has a duty to obey reasonable orders given by the employer
- an employee has a duty to exercise reasonable care and skill when performing his or her duties
- an employer has a duty to provide a safe system of work and a safe working environment.

Avoiding litigation by good management

I must emphasize that the overriding aim should be to avoid litigation. When practices ask for help with problems concerning their staff they often mistakenly look for legal solutions to problems that are caused simply by a failure to manage staff effectively. For example, a single-handed GP asked if the law could help him to persuade his receptionist to provide him with a cup of tea twice a day, morning and late afternoon. (At the time I met him he was actually making tea twice daily for his receptionist.) Many years earlier that doctor had failed to establish control as a manager when he conceded, only a few days after his receptionist started work, that she need not consider the making of tea part of her job. Ever since then he had dreaded raising the subject for fear of unpleasantness. He hoped that the problem would somehow resolve itself. But the question of who made the tea was just the tip of the iceberg as below the surface their working relations had been unsatisfactory from the outset, and these had deteriorated further over the years. The law as such had little to offer in the way of a remedy. The problem had been allowed to drift on for far too long and it needed more than legal action to put it right.

This example is typical of many cases where BMA advice is sought. It illustrates some of the advantages of a more formal approach to the employment relationship. Such an approach should provide a firm foundation for good working relations. The written contract should also describe the disciplinary procedure that would be invoked if performance in the job was unsatisfactory.

The prescription of a more formal approach to such matters, relying on properly agreed and documented contracts, might be regarded as over-reacting to something of minor importance. But this is simply not so. Poor relations between doctor and receptionist may seriously undermine the doctor's efficiency as a practitioner, and where there are only a few members of staff the problems are often more difficult to handle.

Your legal obligations

A contract of employment exists as soon as an employee proves their acceptance of an employer's terms and conditions of employment by starting work, and both employer and employee are bound by the terms offered and agreed. Often the initial agreement is verbal and not written down. But within two calendar months of an employee starting work the employer must give them a written statement about the main terms of employment with an additional note on disciplinary and grievance procedures.

There is every reason to treat the employment contract as an important legal transaction between the two parties and to document it properly. If this is done the documentation should at least avoid those disputes of interpretation which are simply 'your word against mine'. The written statement should include (or refer to another document containing) the following particulars:

- name of the parties
- date employment began and statement about continuity
- job title and place of work
- pay
- hours
- holiday and holiday pay
- sick pay
- maternity provisions (optional)
- pension arrangements
- retirement policy (optional)
- notice
- health and safety at work policy
- grievance, disciplinary and appeals procedure (although the specific requirement in respect of disciplinary procedures was removed for employers with fewer than 20 staff by the Employment Act 1988, it is advisable for all employers to have one).

Once you get the employment contract right, you have gone a long way towards ensuring that unforeseen disputes do not arise from current employment legislation. This is because the task of preparing and agreeing the contract has made sure that you are complying with current employment law and have not unknowingly acted contrary to it at the outset. In addition, if any dispute should arise and you find yourself having to defend your personnel practices and policies, your position will be greatly strengthened if it can be shown that you acted in good faith and had taken reasonable steps to act in accordance with the law.

Rights of the employee

The main employment rights are summarized below. The list is not comprehensive: a few rights that have limited relevance to general practice have been omitted – for example, those concerned with suspension on medical grounds, the right to receive guaranteed pay and the insolvency of an employer.

Contract of employment

After one month's employment the employee is given the right to a certain minimum period of notice, dependent on length of service, and will usually be entitled to pay during notice. Similarly, after one month's employment the employee is required to give a minimum notice of one week. A contract of employment may allow for longer notice periods than the statutory minimum.

Employers must provide all employees with a written statement of the main terms and conditions of their employment within two calendar months of starting work.

Itemized pay statement

An employer must provide each employee with an itemized pay statement showing gross pay and take-home pay, and the amounts and reasons for all variable deductions. It must show the amount and reason for each fixed deduction or alternatively the total amount of all fixed deductions with the amounts and reasons given in a separate annual statement.

Trade union membership and activities

An employer may not lawfully take any action against an employee for being a member of, or for taking part at an appropriate time in the activities of, an independent trade union. An employer may also not take any action against an employee to compel them to join a non-independent trade union or to compel them to join an independent trade union in a closed shop if the employee genuinely objects to membership on grounds of conscience or other deeply held personal convictions.

Time off work

Time off for trade union duties and activities

An employee who is an *office holder* of an independent trade union that is recognized by the employer must be allowed reasonable time off with pay to carry out trade union duties if these are concerned with industrial relations between the employer and the employees. An employee who is a *member* of an independent trade union that is recognized by the employer is entitled to reasonable time off for certain trade union activities. The employer is not obliged to pay the employee for time off for trade union activities.

Time off for public duties

An employer is also required, under certain circumstances, to permit any employee who holds certain public positions reasonable time off to perform these duties. This covers such offices as Justice of the Peace; member of a local authority; member of any statutory tribunal; and member of certain health, education, water or river authorities. The employer is not obliged to pay the employee for the time off for public duties.

Redundancy and time off to look for work

An employee who is being made redundant and who has been continuously employed by the employer for at least two years is entitled to take reasonable time off with pay to look for another job or to make arrangements for training for future employment.

Time off for antenatal care

Any employee who is pregnant may not be unreasonably refused time off with pay to attend appointments for antenatal care. Other than in the case of the first appointment during the pregnancy, an employer is entitled to see a certificate from a registered medical practitioner, midwife or health visitor stating that the employee is pregnant, and to see evidence of the appointments.

Rights of the expectant mother

The right to 14 weeks' maternity leave

This important right applies to all women employees irrespective of length of service or number of hours worked per week.

The right to return to a job

A woman who is expecting a baby and who has worked for her employer continuously for at least two years has the right not to be dismissed because of pregnancy, unless her condition makes it impossible for her to do the job adequately or her continued employment would be against the law. (In these circumstances she must be offered a suitable alternative job if one is available.)

The rights to receive statutory maternity pay and to return to work

To have the right to statutory maternity pay an employee must have at least 26 weeks' recent continuous employment up and into the 15th week before the expected week of confinement, normal weekly earnings of not less than the National Insurance lower limit and have given 21 days' prior notice of intended absence and provided evidence of confinement. Employees paying reduced rate National Insurance contributions, part-timers and 'casual' or temporary staff are also entitled to maternity pay if they satisfy these conditions. Maternity pay is payable once an employee has stopped work if she satisfies the above conditions. It is paid for 18 weeks from any date between the 11th and 6th week before the expected date of confinement.

An employee has the right to return to her former job (or suitable alternative work) at any time before the end of 29 weeks beginning with the week in which her child is born if she satisfies the following conditions:

- she must have been continuously employed for at least two years immediately before the beginning of the 11th week before the expected date of confinement
- she must continue to be employed (whether or not she is actually attending work) until immediately before the beginning of the 11th week before the expected week of confinement
- she must normally tell the employer, in writing, at least 21 days before her maternity absence or as soon as is reasonably practicable, that she is leaving to have a baby, the expected week of confinement and that she intends to return to work.

She may not have the right to return if:

- the employer has five or fewer employees and can show that it is not reasonably practicable for her to be taken back or
- her former job is no longer there because of redundancy and there is no suitable alternative.

Furthermore, the employer may request (not earlier than 49 days before the end of the maternity leave period) written confirmation of her intention to return. This request should be in writing and warn that failure to write back within 14 days or a reasonably practicable period of receipt will debar the right to return. The right to return may be exercised at any time up to 29 weeks beginning with the week in which the child was born. The date of return may be extended beyond this in certain specified instances.

Nevertheless, the right to return shall not apply where the total number of employees did not exceed five at the time immediately before the maternity absence began *and* it was not reasonably practicable for the employer to permit her to return.

Finally, any employer who takes on a temporary replacement for an employee who has stopped work to have a baby should advise the replacement (in writing, at the time of engagement) that the employment will be terminated when the original employee returns.

Unfair dismissal

Employees have the right not to be unfairly dismissed, and employees who think they have been unfairly dismissed may seek a remedy by complaining to an industrial tribunal.

Redundancy pay

Employers are required to make a lump sum compensation payment, called a 'redundancy payment', to employees with at least two years' continuous service who are dismissed because of redundancy. The amount is related to the employee's age, length of service with the employer and weekly pay and is subject to a statutory maximum based on a multiple of an upper limit of a week's pay.

Sex, race and disability discrimination

It is unlawful for any employer to discriminate on grounds of sex or against married persons. It is also unlawful to discriminate on racial grounds, i.e. on grounds of race, colour, nationality (including citizenship) or ethnic or national origins. More recently, it has been made unlawful to discriminate against disability in the field of employment. Employers are prohibited from discriminating in recruitment and in relation to existing employees – for example, in training and promotion.

Equal pay

Employers are required to afford equal treatment to men and women who are employed on 'like work', i.e. work rated as equivalent and work of equal value. Equal pay is, therefore, not restricted to remuneration alone but includes all terms of a contract of employment other than those relating to death or retirement benefits.

Remedies available to employees

The remedy for an alleged breach of contract has lain traditionally with the civil courts; however, new legislation extends the jurisdiction of industrial tribunals to include claims for breaches of employment contracts. Where written statements of the terms and conditions of employment are concerned the remedies lie with industrial tribunals. The tribunal has the power to determine only what particulars the written statement shall include: it cannot arbitrate where any of the particulars is in dispute. Such cases are dealt with by the civil courts. The various remedies for unfair dismissal have been explained above.

An important area where a breach of contract claim may arise concerns any failure on the part of an employer to follow a contractual procedure, e.g. for disciplinary action and dismissal.

Remedies under all the other provisions outlined above lie with industrial tribunals, and in some cases where an employer is found not to have complied with one or more of the provisions, the tribunal may make an award of compensation to be paid by the employer to the employee.

How to introduce a written contract

Once it has been decided to issue written contracts to staff there is a risk of acting hastily and thereby causing unnecessary anxiety. It is important not to upset staff who have served the practice loyally over many years by suddenly asking them to sign and exchange written contracts. A useful approach might be to treat the whole exercise as something which was being 'imposed' on the practice from outside. The next stage is to consider in detail what the written contract should contain, bearing in mind the draft document presented below. Some points may be unclear, and it may be necessary to clarify the details of certain terms and conditions of service – for example, sick leave and holiday provisions. What often emerges is that between the terms and conditions of different staff there are inexplicable variations, which have evolved on an ad hoc basis. In Chapter 7 I explain how you can best change the terms and conditions of an existing contract.

Draft contract of employment

Part I of this statement sets out particulars of the terms and conditions agreed between:

I/We, Dr(s) .... (name)

of .... (address)

and you .... (name)

.... (address)

on .... (date)

Part II sets out the disciplinary procedure, whom you should contact if you wish to appeal against a disciplinary decision or to take up a grievance, and the subsequent steps to be followed in the disciplinary and grievance procedure.

Your employment began on ...
Your employment with your previous employer does not count as part of your continuous period of employment.

Part I

Job title

Receptionist.

Place of work

Your normal place of work is x surgery, but you may be expected to work occasionally at y and z branch surgeries.

Salary

Your salary is ... per annum, payable in arrears on ... every month and your equivalent hourly rate is ...

(London Weighting Allowance is also payable at the appropriate level to those staff covered by agreements of the Administrative and Clerical Staffs Whitley Council.)

The agreement may be seen at ... Your salary is reviewed annually.

Incremental date

Your incremental date is ... and payment of your first increment is due on ...

Hours of work

Your basic hours of work are 36 per week, your normal hours of attendance are ... (A detailed account of a rota arrangement may be required here.) In addition to these hours occasional Saturday morning surgeries will have to be covered on a rotation basis – an arrangement in which all members of staff are required to participate. The salary is calculated to allow for this extra duty and no overtime payments for these sessions will be made. Staff will be required to work overtime occasionally at the request of a doctor – for example, when colleagues are on holiday or are ill extra hours may have to be worked to cover the opening time of the surgery.

Overtime payment

Additional overtime payment will be made at the rate normally paid for an hour's work.

Annual leave

You are entitled to four weeks' paid annual leave, which is normally taken between Easter and Christmas of each year. Reasonable notice must be given of your intention to take leave, and all leave must be arranged with the doctor in charge so that there is adequate cover for the surgery.

Leave must be taken by the end of the calendar year and may not be accumulated from one year to the next unless by prior agreement. Leave entitlement is calculated at the rate of one twelfth of a full year's entitlement for each month of completed service during the first year of employment or during the year of resignation – for example, 3 February to 1 March would equal one month. If a member of staff has anticipated his or her leave entitlement before termination an appropriate deduction may be made from any payment owing.

Bank holidays

The surgery will be closed on official bank and public holidays and any proclaimed national holidays. Payment for these days will be at the normal rate.

Sick leave

If you are entitled to statutory sick pay this will be paid by the employer.

Your entitlement under the practice's own sick pay scheme (which may be revised or withdrawn at its discretion) in any 12 month period is as follows:

Period of continuous service	Basic salary*	Basic half salary*
Less than 6 months	Nil	Nil
Over 6 months to 12 months	Nil	1 month
Over 12 months to 2 years	1 month	2 months
Over 2 years to 5 years	2 months	2 months
Over 5 years	2 months	4 months

Any payment under the statutory sick pay scheme will be offset against your entitlement under the scheme.

Notification of absence because of sickness must be made as early as possible on the first day of sickness. If the absence continues beyond seven working days a medical certificate should be submitted. A self-certification form should be completed for any sickness absence lasting for seven days or less. If the illness lasts for more than seven calendar days you must first notify your absence and also request a self-certification form which should be posted to the practice at the end of the first week of absence.

Any accident or injury arising out of your employment must be reported immediately to the doctor on duty.

*If you are entitled to receive any National Insurance benefits the following deductions will be made from an allowance equal to full basic salary, irrespective of whether you register a claim. So you are advised to ensure that you claim all your entitlements under these Acts:
• the amounts of statutory sickness or invalidity benefits recoverable, if appropriate
• the amount of statutory injury benefit receivable, if appropriate
• the amount of earnings-related supplement to sickness and injury benefit receivable under the National Insurance Acts, if appropriate.

Maternity leave

Subject to length of service and certain other conditions, as laid down in the relevant legislation, women employees are entitled to statutory maternity pay, maternity leave and to return to a job. A certificate of confinement and due notice in writing of maternity absence and return to work, or both, should be provided as required in the legislation.

Pension scheme

Your appointment is superannuable unless you opt out of the NHS pension scheme. Your pensionable salary is subject to deduction of superannuation contributions in accordance with the provisions of the scheme. The NHS pension scheme is contracted out of the State Earnings Related Pension Scheme.

Retirement policy

The normal age of retirement is 60 years and any extension of employment beyond this age is subject to the agreement of both the employee and the practice.

Notice of termination of employment

You are required to give written notice of your intention to terminate your employment and you are entitled to receive in writing the same minimum period of notice. This period of notice is calculated as follows:

- you are entitled to receive one week's notice of termination, increasing to two weeks after two years' service. Thereafter your notice entitlement and requirement will increase by one week for each additional complete year of service up to a maximum of 12 weeks for 12 years' service or longer
- by mutual agreement the period of notice may be varied. Payment in lieu of notice may be made.

Health and safety at work

The practice's policy on health and safety at work is to provide as safe and healthy working conditions as possible and to enlist the support of its employees towards achieving these ends.

Although the overall responsibility rests with the employer, all staff have a legal duty to take reasonable care to avoid injury to themselves or to others in their work activities, and not to interfere with or misuse any clothing or equipment provided to protect health and safety.

The main hazards that staff should be aware of are:

- medical instruments etc. in the consulting room
- prams, bicycles etc.

Any accident to a member of staff or a member of the public should be reported immediately to the practice manager. A factual statement covering to the fullest possible extent all the circumstances of the accident may be required to ascertain the cause to prevent its recurrence.

Part II

Disciplinary procedure

Disciplinary rules and procedures are necessary for promoting fairness and order in the treatment of individuals. They also assist a practice to operate effectively. Rules set standards of conduct and performance at work; procedure helps to ensure that the standards are adhered to and provides a fair method of dealing with alleged failures to observe them.

Disciplinary procedures should not be viewed primarily as a means of imposing sanctions. They should also be designed to emphasize and encourage improvements in individual conduct.

Individuals will be informed of the complaints against them and be given an opportunity to state their case before decisions are reached. They have a right to be accompanied by a colleague at all stages in the procedure. Any written warning given in this procedure will be deemed to have lapsed after one year (and verbal warnings after six months), subject to satisfactory conduct.

The following disciplinary procedure will apply:

- *counselling* – if there is thought to be cause for action under this disciplinary procedure you will first be asked to attend to discuss the matter with the practice manager. The proceedings will not be recorded. It is hoped that this informal counselling will resolve any possible difficulties and lead to the required improvement
- *verbal warning* – if after this there is continued cause for concern there will be a further meeting with the practice manager. You will have an opportunity to state your case. You may be accompanied by a colleague. If after this disciplinary action is deemed appropriate, a verbal warning will be given. The warning will state the nature of the misconduct, specify the disciplinary action being taken, indicate the likely consequences of committing misconduct again, and state, if appropriate, the period of time given for improvement
- *written warnings* – if after this there is continued cause for concern, a formal written warning will be given by the practice manager stating the nature of the complaint and that if no improvement is forthcoming it may result in your dismissal. A second final written warning will be given before dismissal

- *dismissal* – if there is no improvement you may then be dismissed
- *appeal* – there is a right of appeal against dismissal to a doctor who has not been directly involved in the disciplinary action
- *serious misconduct* – there are varying degrees of seriousness of misconduct, so this procedure may be started at any stage depending on the severity of the misconduct. A few examples of gross misconduct that would justify summary dismissal without prior warning are theft, abuse of medicines and a serious breach of confidentiality. This list is not comprehensive. In some circumstances where serious misconduct is thought to have occurred the member of staff concerned may be suspended on full basic salary pending an investigation and a hearing.

Grievance procedure

If you have any grievance relating to your employment you should raise this with the practice manager. Minor grievances may be raised orally, but serious grievances must be in writing.

Signed .... for the practice

This .... day of ....

I acknowledge receipt of this contract of employment and agree to be bound by it. I understand that you retained a copy of this signed contract.

Signed .... employee

This .... day of ....

Notes on the draft contract

At the time of writing it seems likely that the Government will reduce the length of service threshold for unfair dismissal from two years to one year.

1 *Date of contract*. Fill in date when contract is signed. The date employment begins, for example, may be important because various employment rights depend on continuity of service. The date must therefore take account of any employment with a previous employer that counts towards a period of continuous employment by the present employer. In general practice it is very rare for previous employment to count for this purpose.

Box 3.1

There are legal provisions which protect the employment rights of staff in the event of a partnership change or dissolution or where a single-handed GP retires from the list. In deciding whether the staff have a right to continue to be employed, the basic question is whether there has been a 'business transfer'. In answering the question many factors such as the sale of equipment or premises and the continued employment of other staff are highly relevant. Decided cases clearly indicate that the transfer of the goodwill in a business is of great significance. It is likely therefore that any practice assuming responsibility for the list of patients formerly cared for by another practice will take on the responsibilities for employing the staff of the former practice.

---

2 *Employer.* The full name and address of the employer(s) should appear in this space. Contracts should not be provided for staff who are not in fact employed by the practice, such as health authority staff attached to a practice.

3 *Title of job.* It is important that this should adequately describe the scope of the job as the employee otherwise may be justified in maintaining that the work they are asked to do is inconsistent with the job.

4 *Previous period of employment.* The provisions of a contract with regard to the previous period of employment are important whenever the employee has been in the practice longer than the employer(s). This is because under current employment protection and the transfer of undertakings legislation, when a practice is transferred from one doctor to another the period of employment of an employee in the practice at the time of the transfer would normally count as a period of employment with the transferee and the transfer does not break the continuity of the period of employment.

Thus, whereas a practice which takes on a new employee will incur very few obligations during the first two years, it is only at the end of this period that, for example, the employee becomes entitled to compensation if unfairly dismissed unless the dismissal is for an inadmissible reason. But if the employer takes over a practice in which the employee has already worked for, say, 10 years then even on the second day of the practice the employer will not be able to dismiss the employee without paying compensation based on the full 10 years' employment.

5 *Holidays.* The parties are free to make their own arrangements in this regard. In small practices one of the most frequent sources of difficulty concerns staff who are unable to arrange their holidays so that they do not coincide. A possible solution is to provide that in the event of such coincidence the employer shall decide when the holiday will be taken.

6 *Sickness or injury.* Apart from statutory sick pay, employment legislation does not require the employer to pay any statutory minimum in respect of periods of sickness or injury. An industrial tribunal would, however, endorse any right that the employee acquires under a contract of employment.

7 *Pensions.* Anyone employed by the practice to assist in providing general medical services is eligible to join the NHS pension scheme. This includes employees who do not have direct patient contact, such as cleaners and gardeners.

8 *Retirement policy.* It is important to establish a retirement policy well in advance of any particular individual's likely date of retirement.

9 *Notice.* The periods of notice recommended are the statutory minima.

10 *Discipline.* The law provides that the contract of employment should tell an employee where details of the disciplinary procedure and rules governing an appeal against disciplinary action are to be found. Although employers with less than 20 employees are exempt from this requirement, it is nevertheless advisable to provide one. It should be noted that it is increasingly common for employees with less than two years' service to bring breach of contracts claims to industrial tribunals on the grounds that the employer has not followed the disciplinary and dismissal procedure incorporated in the employment contract.

11 *Grievance procedure.* The law also provides that the contract must describe the grievance procedure.

Job description

This should normally be a separate and distinct document from the contract itself. It should set out the main tasks of the job, but also include the mundane tasks – for example, doing the filing or making tea or coffee – which employees sometimes prefer to forget or neglect.

Appendix

Employment right	Qualifying length of service for all employees
Not to be dismissed or discriminated against on grounds of pregnancy, maternity, marital status, sex, colour, race, nationality, ethnic and national origins and disability	No threshold – from first day of employment
Unfair dismissal protection	2 years
Statutory redundancy payments	2 years
Written statement of employment particulars – for example, a contract of employment	2 years
Itemized pay statement	No threshold – from first day of employment
Return to work after 14 weeks' of maternity leave	No threshold – from first day of employment
Return to work after 40 weeks' of maternity leave	2 years
Written statement of reasons for dismissal	2 years
Time off for trade union duties and activities	No threshold – from first day of employment
Time off for public duties	No threshold – from first day of employment
Time off to look for work or arrange training in a redundancy situation	2 years
Guaranteed payments	1 month
Notice of dismissal	1 month
Payment on medical suspension	1 month

Note: At the time of writing it seems likely that the Government will soon reduce the qualifying length of service from two years to one year.

4 Fixed term contracts

Contracts to undertake a specific task • Contracts contingent upon some future event • Contracts specifying an end date • Dismissing a replacement employee

Where to obtain advice and assistance
BMA members should contact their local BMA office.

It should be noted that at the time of writing it seems likely that the Government will reduce the length of service threshold for unfair dismissal from two years to one year.

Temporary employment continues to increase throughout the economy, as employers seek to increase the flexibility of their workforce and to avoid the exigencies of employment legislation; general practice is no exception. Temporary work can take various forms, including seasonal and casual work, employees covering maternity or sickness absence, employment agency staff and employees working under various types of fixed term contracts.

There is no legal definition as such of temporary employment. In practice, temporary employees are normally those workers whose length of service precludes them from most statutory rights and who are usually excluded from sick pay and pension provisions. However, recent legislation has improved the position of temporary employees somewhat by requiring employers to provide a written employment contract within eight weeks of starting work which states how long the temporary work is expected to last or, if it is for a fixed term, the date when it will end.

An increasing number of practices have contemplated introducing temporary and fixed term contracts for at least some of their staff. In part this was an understandable reaction to the growing uncertainties caused by the NHS internal market, the political vagaries associated with fund-holding and the increased discretion exercised by health authorities over reimbursements under the practice staff scheme. There are important advant-ages and disadvantages of fixed term contracts which are summarized in Boxes 4.1 and 4.2. These must be carefully assessed before opting for a type of contract which may be inappropriate to most practices' needs or circumstances.

Box 4.1: Advantages of fixed term contract

- Employee knows from outset that the job is temporary
- Allows short-term projects
- Allows a practice to shed staff if health authority reduces direct reimbursement
- Eliminates the possibility of lengthy and expensive industrial tribunal proceedings
- Appropriate to specialist employees working on a project with a definite end point, e.g. building and construction industries

---

Box 4.2: Disadvantages of fixed term contract

- Encourages short-term perspective among employees which may not be conducive to long-term planning
- Reduces commitment to the practice
- Adversely affects long-term career development and motivation
- Can be legal complexities in drawing up and renegotiating contracts
- Difficult to vary contractual terms during fixed term period
- Termination before expiry date can be difficult and expensive
- Experienced staff with essential skills may be lost at expiry of contract
- Staff tend to concentrate on finding their next job towards the end of a fixed term
- Unusual for clerical and administrative staff earning modest salaries

The law is complicated enough in relation to employment matters. However, because the legal provisions relating to fixed term contracts are particularly complex, a practice should always obtain expert advice from its BMA local office before introducing this type of contract.

There are three main types of fixed term contract:

- contracts which are 'discharged', i.e. completed, by the performance of a certain task or activity, e.g. inputting certain data on to a computer
- contracts whose termination is conditional on the occurrence or otherwise of some specific future event, e.g. the ending of the fundholding scheme
- contracts which specify a termination date, e.g. a one or two year period.

Contracts to undertake a specific task

This type of contract is most appropriate for a 'one-off' project on which staff are specifically employed. When it is completed the contract ends automatically; no notice is required because, to use the correct terminology, the contract has been 'discharged by performance'. Unfair dismissal and redundancy simply do not apply. It is usually advisable to make explicit provision for early termination, i.e. dismissal, before the task is completed in case this should be required to deal with substantial work reduction or unsatisfactory behaviour.

Contracts contingent upon some future event

A key condition for this type of contract to be acceptable to an industrial tribunal is that the future event or non-event must not be subject to the influence of either party to the contract and there must be a clear demonstrable connection between the event or non-event and the continuation of the job.

Contracts specifying an end date

This is the most common type of fixed term contract; an agreement is made at the outset that the contract will end on a specific date. Neither party has to give notice of termination because it simply expires on the specified date. However, if either party is likely to wish to end the contract at an earlier date, it is possible to do so by including a specific clause enabling either party to give notice of termination before the due date.

If the fixed term contract does not include this clause, an employer who ends the contract prematurely may be liable to pay damages equal to the unpaid remuneration for the outstanding period of the contract, which may be a substantial sum.

Some employers have tried to avoid their obligations under employment law by employing staff on a series of fixed term contracts, believing that because each contract was for less than two years these employees were denied the right to complain of unfair dismissal by being prevented from crossing the critical two year threshold. However, this loophole is closed by a legal provision that if a fixed term contract expires without being renewed, a dismissal is deemed to have occurred. Thus, the employee on this type of contract has the same right as any other dismissed employee to compensation for unfair dismissal or redundancy. Moreover, a succession of renewable fixed term contracts, e.g. a series of three one-year contracts, will normally be regarded as comprising a period of continuous employment when assessing eligibility for such compensation, and the employee on fixed term contracts will be treated in the same way as a permanent employee.

An employee can waive their unfair dismissal rights if the fixed term contract is for a single term of one year or more. The existence of this one year threshold is somewhat anomalous, given that the qualifying period for dismissal claims was increased from one to two years many years ago. An employee can also agree to waive their right to redundancy payments, as well as their unfair dismissal rights.

These waivers are only valid if in writing and agreed to by the employee prior to the end of the contract and they only apply at the actual end point of the contract. Waiver clauses do not apply at any intermediate point if an employer opts to terminate the contract early. Every time the fixed term contract is renewed the waiver clause must also be renewed.

Box 4.3 summarizes the main features of this type of contract.

Before opting to appoint staff on a fixed term contract it is vital to weigh its advantages and disadvantages against the needs and circumstances of your practice. And if you should opt to employ someone on this basis, the following information must be made clear in the letter of appointment to the prospective employee:

- when or how the contract expires, i.e. the termination date, task to be completed or the event or non-event that would end the contract
- the nature of any waiver clauses relating to unfair dismissal and/or redundancy.

> **Box 4.3: Main features of fixed term contracts**
>
> - A fixed term contract may be for any length but it must have an identifiable termination date
> - If no period of notice is included, a guarantee of employment (or at least receipt of salary) for the fixed term is implied
> - Non-renewal of a fixed term contract constitutes a dismissal
> - Right to claim unfair dismissal and redundancy payments may be waived if:
>   - contract is for a fixed term of one year or more (for unfair dismissal) or two years or more (for redundancy payments)
>   - dismissal only consists of the fixed term expiring
>   - a written disclaimer is freely and voluntarily agreed to by the employee before contract expires

The information should be clearly explained in a letter of appointment which should also include the main terms and conditions of the job. The prospective employee should also be asked to confirm in writing that their acceptance of the job is based on these conditions.

Dismissing a replacement employee

A temporary replacement employee can be fairly dismissed if they are told in writing at the time of recruitment that the employment will end when the other employee resumes work after an absence wholly or partly because of pregnancy or childbirth.

Complications can arise if the replacement employee is also pregnant at the time of the dismissal and the European Court has ruled that a dismissal in these circumstances is unfair because it amounts to automatic sex discrimination.

5   Employed or self-employed?

Where to obtain advice and assistance

BMA members should contact their local BMA office. Your tax office, local tax enquiry centre or social security office may also be approached for advice.

Because so many employment rights only apply to employees, the distinction between 'employees' and the 'self-employed' can be crucial. Indeed, in order to avoid the impact of the ever growing plethora of employment law, some employers have deliberately opted to redesignate their employees as 'self-employed', sometimes without the expressed consent of the staff concerned. Although the intentions of both parties themselves may be relevant, the courts and the taxation authorities will inevitably assess the nature of the actual contractual relationship to determine whether in fact an individual's status is that of an employee or a self-employed person.

Employment legislation defines an employee as 'an individual who has entered into or works under a contract of employment' and a contract of employment is defined as a 'contract of service or apprenticeship'. In themselves these definitions are not enough to determine whether someone is employed under a contract of service or is self-employed and therefore works under a contract for services. In most instances it is self-evident to which category an individual belongs. But there are areas where genuine uncertainty exists and others where both parties have deliberately opted for self-employed status, either because of the mutual benefits it bestows or because the employer wishes to avoid the obligations of employment legislation. Because there are genuine grey areas the taxation authorities and courts have developed a number of tests to identify employee status.

The Inland Revenue view

The Inland Revenue lists a series of questions which should help to determine an individual's employment status (*see* Boxes 5.1 and 5.2).

Box 5.1: Employee status

If the individual can answer 'yes' to these questions they are probably employed.

- Do you yourself have to do the work rather than hire someone else to do it for you?
- Can someone tell you at any time what to do or when and how to do it?
- Are you paid by the hour, week or month? Can you get overtime pay?
- Do you work set hours or a given number of hours a week or month?
- Do you work at the premises of the person you work for or at a place or places he or she decides?

Box 5.2: Self-employed status

If the individual can answer 'yes' to these questions they are probably self-employed.

- Do you have the final say in how the business is run?
- Do you risk your own money in the business?
- Are you responsible for meeting the losses as well as taking the profits?
- Do you provide the main items of equipment you need to do your job, not just the small tools many employees provide for themselves?
- Are you free to hire other people on your own terms to do the work you have taken on? And do you pay them out of your own pocket?
- Do you have to correct unsatisfactory work in your own time and at your own expense?

The Inland Revenue stresses that if an individual has more than one job or works for several different people for a few days or weeks at a time, these questions have to be answered for each job. Thus, if an individual is self-employed in one job this does not necessarily mean they will be self-employed in any other job; someone can obviously be employed and self-employed at the same time in different jobs.

Similarly, in relation to part-time or temporary work, even though someone does not enjoy the benefits normally associated with full-time employment such as paid holidays, sick pay and a pension scheme, and may even have more freedom to choose their hours of work, unless they can answer 'yes' to all the questions in Box 5.2 the Inland Revenue will normally consider them as employed.

The industrial tribunals' and courts' view

Traditionally legal disputes about whether someone was employed or self-employed have been resolved by applying various tests.

- *The control test*. This refers to the degree of control an employer exercises over a worker; the greater the control, the more likely it is that the worker is an employee. The concept of control includes powers such as the exercise of discipline and dismissal, the fixing of hours or times worked and determining when holidays may be taken.
- *The personal service test*. This focuses on whether an individual is obliged to do the job personally or whether they can delegate it to a substitute.
- *The organizational test*. This requires the following question to be answered: is the worker part and parcel of the organization? A positive response means that the individual would be regarded as an employee.

These single factor tests have been overtaken by industrial tribunals and courts adopting a more flexible approach which relies upon considering a range of factors, including the three referred to above. In short, they are expected to consider all relevant factors and to ask whether a person is in business on their own account. If the answer is 'no' then the individual will normally be deemed an employee.

Among the other factors industrial tribunals and courts consider are the following:

- *Mutuality of obligation*. In a contract of service this usually means that the employer is obliged to provide work and the employee is obliged to accept the work being offered. Problems can arise with this 'mutuality' test if someone is a casual employee, though normally there should be little difficulty in determining whether such obligations actually exist.

- *Financial factors*. For someone to be in business on their own account they should normally carry the financial risk of the business. The following types of payment arrangements are often associated with self-employment: profit (and loss) sharing; lump sum payment 'by the job'; and remuneration based solely on commission. On the other hand, a regular salary (together with provision for holiday and sick pay) is strong prima facie evidence of employment status.

Other factors considered by tribunals and courts include:

- whether an individual is able to perform services for others whilst working for a particular employer
- whether an employer is able to discipline and dismiss someone
- the custom and practice in that type of work, industry or profession.

A note of caution

An increasing number of practices are currently considering moving staff from 'employed' to 'self-employed' status. This change is being considered for a variety of motives, including the practice's desire to avoid its obligations as an employer which derive from employment protection law, e.g. protection against unfair dismissal, redundancy rights and maternity rights. However, it should be remembered that protection against sexual, racial and disability discrimination applies to all workers, employed and self-employed. This desire to escape the rigours of employment law has been greatly strengthened in recent years as a result of major changes in the law which have substantially increased the rights of part-timers and expectant mothers. However, even if the employee is quite willing to collude in this change to self-employed status, it cannot be over-emphasized that it will be challenged by the tax authorities if they suspect that there has been no genuine change in contractual arrangements. A self-employment arrangement must be entered into in good faith and not for the purpose of defrauding the Inland Revenue, otherwise the contract will be deemed to be totally void and will be unenforceable.

Finally, if you or the employee are unsure whether their status is that of an employee or a self-employed person, you may contact your local tax enquiry centre, tax office or social security office for advice. They will be only too willing to assist and will give you a written decision on your employee's employment status. If you wish to dispute their decision, you can appeal against it. Normally, a decision taken by one Government department will be accepted by the other, if it is provided with all the facts at the time and the circumstances remain the same.

6 GP registrar contracts

The need for a contract • The BMA model contract • Resolving disputes

Where to obtain advice and assistance

Advice about training for general practice is provided by regional advisers in general practice and the Joint Committee on Postgraduate Training for General Practice or the RCGP. (Both the Joint Committee and RCGP can be contacted at 14 Princes Gate, London SW7 1PU.)

BMA members should contact their local BMA office for advice and assistance, particularly in relation to problems concerning removal expenses. The GMSC has prepared a model contract for GP registrars, which can be obtained from local offices.

The need for a contract

Surprisingly, many GP trainers still fail to provide their registrars with written employment contracts, relying instead on verbal agreements. However, they are legally obliged to provide a written contract within eight weeks of a GP registrar starting work.

This written statement needs to include details of, or refer to another document that specifies, the following:

- name of parties
- job title
- start date of employment and statement about continuity
- notice
- place of work

- pay
- pension
- hours
- holiday and holiday pay
- sick pay.

The reasons trainers forget or neglect to provide registrars with written employment contracts are many and varied. First, the registrars are often employed for such a short time, it becomes a question of 'why bother?'. Second, with most registrars' terms and conditions agreed nationally with little room for local variations, a detailed written contract may seem unnecessary. A third reason is that GPs generally neglect such matters, including their own partnership deeds.

The BMA model contract

The advice provided below is based on the current version of a model contract prepared by the BMA General Medical Services Committee with assistance from its GP registrars subcommittee. It can be varied as long as variations are agreed and freely entered into by both parties. BMA members can get a comprehensive model contract from their local BMA office.

Although registrars may receive tuition from several members of the partnership or group, they will normally be in contract with the trainer. Therefore only one principal's name needs to be included in the contract. When the trainer goes on holiday, another principal should be nominated to carry out these duties under the terms of this contract.

At this point in the contract it should be stated that both parties must be registered with the General Medical Council and should be members of medical defence bodies, at their own expense.

The contract should say that the trainer is employing the registrar for the purpose of vocational training for a specified number of months from a named date. It should also state that the registrar's place of work is at the practice's main surgery, at a given address, and in its branch surgery, at a given address.

Included in the agreement should be a point that allows the contract to be terminated by the registrar or trainer, if either gives one month's written notice.

Details about pay and pensions, and regulations regarding hours of work should all be clearly defined in the contract. The advice below suggests which points need to be raised in the agreement and offers guidance on the rules surrounding pay and hours.

The registrar's salary and car allowance should be paid at the rates specified in the Red Book. Payments should be made in arrears at the end of each completed calendar month.

The registrar will be subject to the NHS superannuation rules and the trainer should deduct from the registrar's salary contributions due under the NHS pension scheme.

The registrar's hours of work in the practice, the training programme and regular periods of tuition and assessment should be agreed between the trainer and the registrar. They should take account of day-release courses and any other commitments recommended by the local general practice advisory committee.

The registrar's hours of work in the practice – during and outside normal hours – should not exceed the average hours of work of full-time partners and should not exceed 56 hours of continuous duty, day shifts followed by on-call.

If the registrar is absent because of sickness, the trainer should continue to pay the salary and allowances as required by the Red Book. Any payment received from the statutory sick pay scheme will be off-set against these payments.

The trainer should be told of any absence due to sickness on the first day of illness. A self-certification form should be completed for any sickness absence lasting for seven days or less. If the illness continues beyond seven days, a medical certificate should be submitted.

Registrars are supernumerary to the usual work of the practice and therefore should not be used by the practice as a substitute for a locum.

Details of holidays and study leave should also be included in the agreement. The registrar is entitled to five weeks' holiday during 12 months, and pro rata for shorter periods, and to statutory and general national holidays or time off in lieu.

The registrar is also entitled to 30 days' approved study leave on full pay, including time at day-release courses, during the 12 months, pro rata for shorter periods. Additional study leave may be agreed between trainer and registrar but this should be approved by the regional adviser.

There are several guidelines for GPs to follow regarding paying registrars in special circumstances. First, a registrar who goes on maternity leave is entitled to be paid by the trainer, if she satisfies the qualifying conditions in the Red Book.

Second, the GP registrar should not be required to undertake work that generates private income for the practice, unless any contrary arrangement has been agreed at the start of the training period. An exception to this rule is if the registrar is required to assist the practice with a fee-earning educational presentation or he or she is required to perform such duties for his or her own educational benefit. Any legacy or gift received by the registrar becomes his or her personal property.

If the GP registrar is elected to represent GP registrars on recognized bodies or to attend the local medical committee's annual conference or special conferences, he or she should be allowed special paid leave for this purpose. The GP registrar should obtain the consent of the trainer for each absence from duty. This consent should not be withheld unless the trainer considers that there are exceptional circumstances for doing so.

The trainer should provide a telephone at the registrar's home, and pay a proportion of the rental and cost of calls that reflect practice use. The trainer should also provide message-taking facilities required by the registrar when on call.

The contract should list those terms that refer to the registrar's method of practice. It should be made clear that the registrar agrees to care and be responsible for any medical equipment and supplies provided by the trainer.

With the trainer's agreement, which should not be unreasonably refused, a registrar may undertake professional activities, whether remunerated or not, outside those of the practice.

The registrar should apply himself or herself diligently to the educational and training programme and the service commitments of the practice.

The contract should state that the registrar will keep records of his or her clinical work in the practice as reasonably required by the trainer. The registrar must also treat matters relating to the practice and its patients confidentially, apart from that information requested by the regional general practice subcommittee.

The registrar must live at an agreed address during the training period.

The contract should say that the registrar will provide, maintain and pay all the running costs of the transport required to carry out efficiently the duties and responsibilities of the post.

For one year after completing the training programme, the registrar, unless practising in the trainer's practice, will not:

- accept on their own NHS list any patient who, during the training programme, was on the NHS lists of the trainer or his or her partners
- attend or treat in the capacity of a GP any patient from the trainer's, or their partners', lists or
- recommend any such patient to seek inclusion on the NHS lists of any GP other than the trainer and their partners.

This only applies to patients who lived within a radius of one mile of the main surgery during the registrar's training.

Resolving disputes

It is rare to include an arbitration clause in a contract. Therefore, the BMA recommends that any dispute between the registrar and trainer concerning the contract or the arrangements under which the registrar is employed, but not the education and training aspects of the job, should be referred, under the 1950 and 1979 Arbitration Acts, to a sole arbitrator nominated by the BMA secretary.

This clause in the GP registrar's model contract reflects its widespread inclusion in GP partnership agreements.

It can offer a point of reference for such disputes, especially for a small-scale employer that does not have the managerial hierarchy of larger organizations. This in itself can provide a framework for grievance, disciplinary and appeals procedures.

Disputes between registrars and trainers can have serious consequences for a young doctor's future career prospects, so it is important to have procedures that resolve a dispute fairly and quickly.

Nevertheless, the arbitration process has its limitations and an arbitrator's services can be costly. The costs are usually shared by the disputing parties.

Any dispute over the registrar's education and training should be referred to the general practice regional adviser who should refer it to the general practice subcommittee of the regional postgraduate education committee, whose decision will be final and binding on both parties.

7 How to change a contract of employment

Nature of the employment contract • Need for consent • If your staff consent to change • A written contract can allow for change • If consent is not forthcoming • A written contract is advisable

Where to obtain advice and assistance

BMA members can obtain advice and assistance from their local BMA office.

Employment contracts are continually changing and developing. Every pay rise requires a variation of the original contract, as does any change in the duties or hours of work of the staff. Although staff may be tolerant of change as such – especially if they benefit from it – some variations in their contracts may meet with strong objections and even resistance.

Some employers have come to believe that they cannot change a contract of employment once it has been agreed with an employee. Others think that because it is a written contract then change is even more difficult to achieve, and in some cases even take the view that this justifies not providing written contracts of employment. In fact, any employer can change employees' contracts, but may subsequently encounter serious difficulties (such as a claim for breach of contract) if the task is approached in the wrong way and does not gain the employee's consent.

Nature of the employment contract

It may be helpful to begin by reminding ourselves what constitutes a contract of employment. First, it is important to remember that a contract exists between a practice and its employees irrespective of whether or not most of it has been encapsulated in a written document. Moreover, even if there is a comprehensive written document the contract of employment when viewed in its entirety also includes unwritten understandings and working practices (which are commonly referred to as 'custom and practice').

The law requires all practices to issue to all employees a statement of the main particulars of employment. The written statement should be issued within two calendar months of the employee's starting work and should include the following information:

- name of the parties
- date employment began and statement about continuity
- job title
- place of work
- pay
- hours
- holiday and holiday pay provisions
- sick pay
- pension
- notice
- grievance, disciplinary and appeals procedures (employers with less than 20 employees are exempt from the specific requirements in respect of the disciplinary procedure).

In addition, it is advisable to include information in the contract on:

- retirement policy
- maternity arrangements.

The law requires that changes in the terms of the main particulars of employment need to be notified to the employee within one month of the change.

The law also requires an employer of five or more staff to issue a written policy statement on health and safety matters as these affect the staff and the arrangements that have been made for carrying out the policy.

The statutory requirement to provide written statements on these matters does not have to be supplemented in any way. There is no legal obligation to provide a written contract as such. But in practice the written statement of the main particulars of employment (together with your policy statement on health and safety matters) can be regarded as the basis of a written contract of employment. The contract as a whole also includes the job description (whether written or not) and the many informal and unwritten understandings and working practices which always form an important part of any employment contract. An example of these informal and unwritten practices are the arrangements normally followed when staff take coffee and tea breaks.

Need for consent

In practice there are various approaches to changing a contract of employment. Whichever approach is adopted the basic principle that must be borne in mind is that an employee should consent to changes before these can become contractually binding, irrespective of whether the consent is implied or by express agreement, given in advance of or at the time of the change. This principle underlies the different ways in which employment terms may be changed.

It is always preferable, if possible, to seek to reach agreement on the proposed changes. Of course, many employees are not favourably disposed towards changes if these affect their duties or hours of work. But sometimes you may be surprised at their receptiveness. Second, it is very important to give clear and defensible reasons for the change. Try to explain why it is necessary in the interests of the good running of the practice. Try to ensure that your reasons are fully understood (even if they are not initially accepted) and never rely on other members of your staff to put your case on your behalf. Often there is nothing more damaging than a second-hand explanation of your intentions, particularly if it is given by someone who is not favourably disposed towards them. Most practices have a small enough group of staff for this personal approach to be practicable.

When you have explained the change, and your reasons for having to introduce it, listen carefully to any reasons your staff may have for not accepting it. It is worth considering carefully how far their objections can be answered. If their reasons for not wanting the change seem reasonable it is well worth taking the time and trouble to examine them to see whether a compromise can be agreed which will satisfy both the needs of the practice and the wishes of staff. At this point you may even find yourself participating in some gentle and informal negotiations. A compromise is often possible and well worth looking for at the outset of the whole exercise. If you aim at a compromise this may lead you to increase marginally the extent of your original proposals, if only to enable you to show your own willingness to compromise.

If your staff consent to change

The crucial consideration when changing an employment contract is the matter of 'consent', and this can be given by an employee in several ways.

Consent given by express agreement

This may be given verbally, but to avoid problems of proof and disputes about who said what and when, it is preferable to obtain such agreement in writing, particularly if the proposed change is a significant one. An employer is, in any case, required to put in writing the term of the contract (as changed) if it relates to any one of those matters listed on p. 55.

If your employee has expressly consented to the change there is usually no doubt that the new term of the contract is contractually binding. It is important to bear in mind that there is a difference between a position where your employee voluntarily accepts a new term and one where it is effectively imposed because the option of declining the proposed change is not a practical possibility. As you may expect, this matter turns on the question of what may be regarded as 'reasonable'. There are no hard and fast rules which can be applied here. What is and is not 'reasonable' depends on the nature of the change, your reasons for introducing it and the circumstances in which it is being implemented.

Consent shown by implied agreement

Implied agreement is normally assumed if your employee continues to work under the new contractual terms without complaint. In fact, it can be established by custom and practice if all the employees affected by the change are fully aware of it and continue to work. For this reason it is most important for an employee to make known any objection without delay and to ensure that the objection is clearly understood by the employer.

A written contract can allow for change

The contract itself may contain provisions that allow for changes in such matters as pay, the place of work, working hours and the duties of the job. In these circumstances the actual change is a matter for the employer or manager to initiate. This arrangement typically applies if the pay of staff is increased annually as a consequence of pay settlements elsewhere in the health service.

The way in which change can be allowed for within the terms of a written contract is by 'broad' drafting. For example, a receptionist's contract may say that their pay is to be determined by reference to a document setting out the rates of pay for National Health Service clerical and

administrative staff. Similarly, the contract might state that the receptionist is required to work at the practice's premises, wherever these may
be located in the practice area. In the job description reference may be
made to 'any other duties of a clerical or administrative nature that may
be required from time to time'.

The overall effect of drafting the contract in this way is to increase your
rights, as the employer or manager, to alter employees' duties, to change
the location where they work and even to vary their hours and shifts. Of
course, on the other side of the equation there is a corresponding loss of
rights for staff.

It is particularly important to note that the job descriptions of staff,
their hours of work and their place of work are three aspects of their
contracts that should be written in a manner which allows for change. It
is too easy for people to presume that the ambit of their contract obligations is the same as the duties they actually perform. This may happen if
staff become accustomed to a more limited range of duties than those originally defined in their contracts and may be avoided if their job descriptions are broadly drafted.

If you have taken care to draft broadly this does not mean that you have
an unfettered right to vary your employees' contracts as you wish. If your
change leads to the sacking of an employee you may find that the industrial
tribunal, in considering an unfair dismissal claim, will wish to examine
whether the change you introduced was reasonable in all the circumstances.

If consent is not forthcoming

It may not be possible to obtain the consent of your staff even if you have
made considerable efforts to agree the change with them. At this stage if
you decide to go ahead and implement the change you should give reasonable notice of your intentions. Ultimately, if you are called to defend your
actions in an industrial tribunal it will be concerned about the extent to
which you have consulted your staff and sought to reach agreement with
them and the reasonableness of your changes in the contracts of employment. Fortunately, tribunals recognize that any business has to be run efficiently, that no business arrangements can remain static and immutable
and that we live in a world where change is regarded as an essential pre-
requisite for survival.

In normal circumstances any change imposed unilaterally by an employer without the consent of the employee will be a breach of contract.
If this is a *fundamental* breach of contract, hitting at the heart of the

contract, the employee may be entitled to claim compensation for constructive dismissal. Furthermore, even if it does not constitute a fundamental breach an employee can claim damages for the breach in a civil court. It is possible (but not always so) to avoid these problems if you give sufficient notice of your intention to introduce the change. It has been thought that the length of notice of the change required is the same as that which would be needed to terminate the contract lawfully. But even if this notice is given the employer could be liable to pay compensation for unfair dismissal or redundancy if the employee still refuses to accept the change and subsequently leaves. The advantage of giving adequate notice of the change is that employees are likely to be left with little or no time to protest after the change has been introduced because they have already had time to think it over.

A written contract is advisable

Chapter 3 emphasized the benefits of having properly documented written contracts for staff. In particular, it recommended practices to satisfy their legal obligations by issuing to staff written statements of the main terms and conditions of service. It is important to remember that a contract of employment exists irrespective of whether it has been expressed in writing. Industrial tribunals do not hesitate to interpret and clarify the terms of an unwritten contract by drawing on a knowledge of verbal understandings and the customs and practices associated with your surgery and its staff. The advantage of a written contract, if properly drafted, is that it clarifies beyond any reasonable doubt the terms of service of staff, including their duties and their hours of work. Furthermore, if the contract is carefully drafted it can allow you to introduce changes without the risk of incurring serious legal difficulties.

There are some practices which have provided their staff with written contracts and now believe that it is difficult, if not impossible, to change these. It must be emphasized that the issues in changing the terms of an employment contract are essentially the same irrespective of whether it is based primarily on a formal written agreement or simply consists of verbal agreements, understandings and customary working practices. It is only the practicalities that differ.

When deciding how to approach the business of varying an employment contract it is vital to recognize that there are no firm guidelines on what is reasonable or unreasonable. We can only point to general principles largely derived from the case law of industrial tribunals.

Finally, there is an important adage that should always be borne in mind at the outset: you must never assume before you start that changes cannot be made. Too often employers are debilitated by their own defeatist attitudes and consequently do not even begin to consider the options available to them.

8 Maternity rights

Time off for antenatal care • The right to 14 weeks' maternity leave
• Pregnancy and childbirth are inadmissible reasons for dismissal
• Right to statutory maternity pay • Right to come back to work •
The return to work • A legal labyrinth

Where to obtain advice and assistance

BMA local offices and local offices of the Government's Advisory,
Conciliation and Arbitration Service (ACAS). On matters concerning
SMP call the Social Security advice line on 0800 393539 or the
Contributions Agency at your local Social Security Office.

Most practices employ only a handful of staff and a high proportion are
women. The employment rights of the expectant mother are both intricate
and stringent. Thus, any employer with few staff may be faced with serious administrative difficulties if a member of staff is pregnant.

Four established employment rights are acquired by an expectant
mother:

- not to be unreasonably refused time off work for antenatal care and to
  be paid when permitted that time off
- to complain of unfair dismissal because of pregnancy or childbirth
- to receive statutory maternity pay
- to return to work with her employer after a period of absence on
  account of pregnancy or confinement.

To these it is necessary to add a fifth comparatively new right:

- to take 14 weeks' maternity leave and to receive statutory maternity pay.

These rights are acquired by all women employees but they are subject to
the conditions and limitations described below. It should be noted that

these rights do not apply to women partners, who are independent contractors.

The following account of the law governing maternity rights is complex. It is intended to serve as a source document to be referred to when the need arises. It is important to note at the outset that there are different qualifying conditions for each maternity right. Because this area of employment law is so complex you should not hesitate to seek expert advice and assistance. BMA members may seek help from their local BMA office.

Time off for antenatal care

Irrespective of how long she has worked in your practice, an employee has the right not to be unreasonably refused time off work to receive antenatal care and to be paid for this time off. To acquire this right the following conditions have to be met. First, she must have made an appointment for antenatal care and the time off must be requested to keep the appointment. Second, except in the case of the request for time off for the first appointment, the employee must, if asked, produce for your inspection both a certificate from a medical practitioner, midwife or health visitor stating that she is pregnant and an appointment card (or some other document) showing that the appointment has been made. Your employee should be paid the appropriate hourly rate for the period of absence from work. Any employee who is improperly denied these rights is entitled to complain to an industrial tribunal. These rights are acquired by any woman as soon as she joins your staff.

The right to 14 weeks' maternity leave

The Trade Union Reform and Employment Rights Act 1993 implemented a European Union directive giving all women employees a right to 14 weeks' maternity leave during which they are eligible to receive a statutory allowance not less than the level of statutory sick pay. Of course, some women employees already enjoy more favourable contractual rights to maternity leave and they will obviously avail themselves of these. However, it is important to note that this new right is universal in its application in that it is not dependent on a woman employee's length of service.

This right to maternity leave is subject to these conditions:

- it starts on the employee's first day of absence from work wholly or partly because of pregnancy or stillbirth
- if this first day of absence is before the beginning of the 11th week before expected date of birth, the employee's maternity leave period starts on the first day on which she is absent after the beginning of the 11th week
- if the birth is before the date when maternity leave actually begins, the leave period starts on the date of birth
- to obtain this right the employee must:
  - tell her employer in writing at least 21 days before her maternity leave period starts or, if this is not reasonably practicable, tell her employer as soon as possible that she is pregnant and the expected date of birth
  - show her employer a certificate giving the expected date of birth.

This right to maternity leave complements the right to return to work in the following way. The right to return to work applies at any time during a period extending from the end of the new statutory maternity leave to 29 weeks after the birth, but is available only to women employees who have been continuously employed for not less than two years.

Pregnancy and childbirth are inadmissible reasons for dismissal

To give effect to the right to 14 weeks' unpaid maternity leave a right was introduced for all women employees, irrespective of their length of service, not to be dismissed on grounds of pregnancy or childbirth. Thus, any woman employee is automatically regarded as having been unfairly dismissed if:

- the reason (or principal reason) for the dismissal relates to her pregnancy
- her maternity leave is ended by the dismissal and the reason for it relates to her childbirth
- her contract of employment is ended after her maternity leave for a reason related to the fact that she benefited from this leave
- she is made redundant during the maternity leave and the special statutory redundancy procedures have not been followed, i.e. offering alternative similar work.

Right to statutory maternity pay

Any woman employed in the same job for 26 weeks is entitled to 18 weeks' statutory maternity pay (SMP). This replaced the previous three tests that led to different rates of maternity pay, depending on whether a woman had worked in the same job for 26 weeks, two years or five years.

The 18 weeks' SMP does not fit neatly with the 14 weeks' maternity leave. Those women who are only entitled to the minimum 14 weeks must return to work when their leave runs out.

Women qualifying for SMP get the higher rate – 90% of earnings for the first six weeks of leave – and the standard rate of SMP for the other 12, which is in line with statutory sick pay.

The statutory maternity allowance is paid to women who do not qualify for SMP. This is paid at the same level as the standard rate of SMP.

If the qualifying conditions are met, an employer cannot avoid paying SMP by claiming that an employee has agreed to forgo entitlement or by requiring the employee to contribute towards its cost. All employers must pay SMP to eligible employees, although it may be paid as part of a larger sum that includes the employer's own maternity pay arrangements.

Right to come back to work

The law defines this general right to maternity leave in terms whereby a woman retains 'the benefit of the terms and conditions of employment which would have been applicable to her if she had not been absent'. Apart from pay, which is specifically excluded, this entitles women to preserve their contractual benefits during the 14 week leave period and it therefore follows that a woman's employment contract continues while she is away on maternity leave during this period. In addition, the law specifically protects all women regardless of length of service against dismissal on account of pregnancy or maternity leave.

The law also preserves the right to return to work for women employees with two years' service who decide to return after taking 40 weeks' maternity leave. The request for written confirmation of a woman's return cannot be made earlier than 21 days before the end of her maternity leave period.

An employee has the right, subject to the limitations outlined below, to her former job at any time before the end of the period of 29 weeks (a week normally means a week ending with Saturday) beginning with the week in which her child is born (the 29 week period may in some circum-stances be extended) and on her return to be employed on terms no less favourable than those that would have applied to her if she had not been absent. (For example, if your staff had received a pay increase during her absence this would also have to be applied to her.)

Several conditions have to be met to acquire this right:

- your employee must have been continuously employed by you for at least two years immediately before the beginning of the 11th week before the expected week of confinement
- your employee must continue to be employed by you (whether or not she is actually coming to work) until immediately before the beginning of the 11th week before the expected week of confinement
- your employee must give the following information to you *in writing* at least 21 days before she begins her maternity absence (or if this is not possible, as soon as is reasonably practicable):
  - that she is away from work to have a baby
  - that she intends to return to work after this absence
  - the expected week of confinement (if the confinement has already occurred, the date of confinement)
- if you asked for a certificate of the expected week of confinement this must be produced.

After the maternity absence has begun the following conditions apply:

- you may send her a written request, not earlier than 21 days before the end of the maternity leave period, asking her to confirm in writing that she intends to return to work. If you write asking for this confirmation you should explain in your letter that she must give confirmation in writing within 14 days of receiving your letter. Again, if this is not pos-sible her confirmation should be given as soon as is reasonably practic-able. If she does not reply confirming her intention to return, the right to return is lost
- she must inform you in writing of the date she intends to return. Some examples of completed written notifications are appended on p. 67.

The return to work

Your employee may choose when to return to work, provided that it is within a period of 29 weeks beginning with the week in which her child was born. If she is ill and produces a medical certificate she may delay her return for a further four weeks from the date she originally gave for

her return or, if she has not notified a date, for up to four weeks from the
end of the 29 week period. She may, however, delay her return to work
only once. You may defer an employee's return to work for up to four
weeks from her notified date provided that you give specified reasons and
inform the employee of the date on which she may return.

If you do not allow your employee to return to her old job this will be
treated as dismissal. Her right to return, however, may be restricted in the
following circumstances:

- if the total number of your employees immediately before the beginning
  of her maternity absence was five or less (including the pregnant employee), and you can show that it is not reasonably practicable for you
  to take her back in her old job (or to offer her suitable alternative work
  – which means work that is both suitable and appropriate for the employee and where the terms, conditions and location are not substantially less favourable than those of the old job) the failure to permit her
  to return will not be treated as a dismissal and any claim of unfair dismissal will fail. But if these circumstances occur the onus of proof lies
  with the employer
- if her former job in the practice is no longer available because of
  redundancy, the Act states you must offer her a suitable alternative job
  if one is available, otherwise the dismissal will be automatically unfair.
  If she unreasonably refuses a suitable offer, however, she may lose her
  right to redundancy pay
- if you can show that it is not reasonably practicable, for a reason other
  than redundancy, to offer your employee her old job back, that you
  have offered a suitable alternative job, and that the employee has subsequently unreasonably rejected the offer (or even accepted it on unreasonable terms) your failure to permit her return to her original job will
  not be treated as a dismissal and any claim of unfair dismissal will fail.
  In these circumstances the onus of proof lies with you as the employer.

Finally, if you employ a temporary replacement you must inform them in
writing that the temporary employment will be terminated on the return
of the employee who is absent because of pregnancy or confinement.

A legal labyrinth

This area of employment law must surely be one of the most complex for
both the employer and employee, and it has become more complicated as
time progresses. I cannot personally apologize for its complexity because

I have had no responsibility for its drafting or its content. For the employer with only a handful of staff, without a personnel manager or personnel department, applying the law requires great care. Any mistake, even if it is wholly due to ignorance or a misunderstanding of the law, could lead to a tribunal case and even a costly award against you. Indeed, it is almost a test of tenacity for both you and your employee to satisfy the requirements of the employment rights of the expectant mother.

It may be helpful to conclude by summarizing these rights. The overall statutory framework of maternity comprises these separate rights, each of which is effectively self-standing and has been enacted as an expedient solution to a specific problem.

The following apply to all employees:

- not to be unreasonably refused paid time off for antenatal care
- not to be dismissed for reasons of pregnancy or childbirth
- to take 14 weeks' maternity leave.

The remaining two rights depend on certain qualifying conditions:

- to return to work after 29 weeks' absence due to pregnancy or childbirth
- to be paid statutory maternity pay.

Appendix: Examples of written notification on the right to return

- Employee's first notification: to be given to the employer at least 21 days before beginning maternity absence (or, if it is not reasonably practicable to do so by that date, as soon as is reasonably practicable afterwards).

Dear Mr Other,
This is to let you know that
1 I am leaving work to have a baby
2 My expected week of confinement is ....
3 I intend to return to work after the baby is born.

Yours sincerely,
Ophelia X

- Employer's request for confirmation of intention to return: to be sent by the employer not earlier than 21 days before the end of the maternity leave period.

Dear Miss X,

This is to ask you whether you still intend to return to work. If you do, I must inform you that you are required to give me confirmation of your intention to return in writing before the date you are due to return. Failure to reply will mean that you will lose your right to return to work with me.

Yours sincerely,
A N Other

• Employee's reply to employer's request for confirmation of intention to return.

Dear Mr Other,

This is to let you know that I still intend to return to work.

Yours sincerely,
Ophelia X

• Employee's final notification: to be sent before proposed date of return.

Dear Mr Other,

This is to let you know that I will be coming back to work on 7 March.

Yours sincerely,
Ophelia X

9 Absence from work

Recognizing patterns of absence • Dealing with long-term sickness • Dealing with short-term sickness • Dealing with unauthorized absences, including lateness • Taking a fair, firm and sympathetic approach

Where to obtain advice and assistance

BMA members should contact their local BMA office. Your local ACAS office can also provide advice.

A practice with a small number of staff can face great difficulty when handling an employee's prolonged or frequent absence. There are several types of absences from work: certificated or uncertificated sick leave; unauthorized absences including lateness; and authorized absences (apart from holidays, absence for public duties, antenatal care, maternity leave and for attending a training course). It may seem presumptuous to advise doctors on how to deal with sickness absence among their staff, but we are all familiar with the proverbial cobbler's children's shoes. Members of any profession or occupation may unknowingly forget or neglect to apply their special knowledge and skills to their own circumstances.

It may be helpful to explain the difference between authorized and unauthorized absences. Employers will decide for themselves the grounds on which absence may be authorized. It is important that you lay down clear rules and that your staff are familiar with these. Your staff should know the limits within which absence is permissible and you should apply these fairly and consistently. For example, different employers will apply different rules to the circumstances when absence may be authorized for a bereavement. Undoubtedly, you will have your views about how much leave is appropriate and in what circumstances it should be allowed and will decide when leave may be authorized for this reason. But it is vital to decide on a policy and apply it consistently.

In any practice the direct and indirect costs of a high level of absence may be considerable and these may include the cost of providing sick pay, paying additional overtime to other staff, employing temporary staff, a reduction in the standards of your services to patients, disruption to working arrangements and a lowering of morale, together with increased dissatisfaction among staff. Thus, it is worth developing and maintaining a procedure to monitor and control absence from work.

Recognizing patterns of absence

There has been research into patterns of absence. Some trends have been found that may alert you to the types of absences to watch for in your practice:

- young people tend to take more frequent and shorter periods of sick leave, and older people longer but less frequent periods
- unauthorized absence may be common among new employees while established employees will have learnt the standards of the practice and know how to follow these (*see* Chapter 2)
- fortunately for general practice, the incidence of absence from work is a far greater problem in large and impersonal organizations but when it occurs in a small organization the effects may be disproportionately disruptive.

It is difficult to deal with absenteeism unless you can establish the facts of each case and have kept adequate records. If all absences are recorded you will be in a better position to identify problem areas and also ensure that any action that you take is fair and reasonable. The principle of consistency may be embodied in the procedure (however informal or simple it may be) that you choose to apply when investigating and dealing with any case of frequent or prolonged absence.

Dealing with long-term sickness

Absence because of long-term illness is almost always a most difficult problem to handle, especially in a small organization. If one of your staff is away sick for a long time or is unable to come to work regularly and consistently because of chronic ill health, you are faced with the unwelcome task of keeping the job open to offer security to your sick employee and thus (it is hoped) aid recovery, and having to maintain the standard of service in the surgery. Your predicament is even greater if the sick employee has had long service with you and occupies a key position in the daily running of the surgery. GPs and their practice managers probably find this dilemma even more intractable than other employers. Not only do they have the good fortune of being blessed with particularly loyal and long-serving staff but their professional calling instils empathy and compassion for chronic ill health. The problem may be compounded if your employee is also a patient on the practice list.

There is obviously no easy answer to this problem and the decision that you finally reach will depend on the circumstances of your practice. It may be helpful, however, to consider these questions if only to ensure that you have assessed the available options.

- Just how much difficulty is being caused by this employee's absence? How long can you manage without a replacement? Can you fill the post satisfactorily temporarily? (Do not forget to ensure that your temporary replacement is aware that the job is temporary.) Can the work be shared or reorganized to accommodate a long-term absence? Are your other staff willing to accept an additional workload or responsibility for a prolonged (and possibly indefinite) period?
- Have you obtained a prognosis from your employee's general practitioner? The law now requires employers to notify employees of such an intention and to obtain consent. (Such a notification must inform employees of their rights under the Act, i.e. to withhold consent, to have access to the report before it is forwarded to the employer and to be able to amend details which they consider incorrect or misleading.) Have you considered seeking an independent medical opinion? Is a full recovery likely or will the employee be unlikely ever to return to the old job? (Particular difficulties may arise if one of the partners is the employee's general practitioner. An obvious conflict of interest may arise and may make the decision more difficult to reach. Although as the employee's own general practitioner you should have full knowledge of the prognosis, it may be advisable to obtain an independent medical opinion before you reach a final decision. In circumstances where this is practicable, adjacent practices have been known to agree an informal arrangement whereby staff are encouraged to register in the neighbouring practice even if they were on one of the practice partners' lists when they originally joined the staff. But such an arrangement is not always feasible, especially in rural areas.)
- Could your employee return to work if special arrangements were made, e.g. could help be given with transport, the work reorganized or the job redesigned?

- Are you likely to have any alternative, lighter or less stressful work available? Would a part-time job be feasible? Could a full-time job be shared?
- The age and length of service of your sick employee will be vital considerations. Would early retirement be a mutually acceptable solution, perhaps with an enhanced pension or an ex gratia payment?
- Can you help the employee to find more suitable employment elsewhere in your locality? The practice may be well placed to give such help.

Whatever conclusion you reach after taking these and any other factors into account, it is most important that the employee is made aware of the position. On medical and humanitarian grounds there may be good reasons for leaving the matter in the air, implying that you will accept the employee back when they have recovered. But this deliberate 'indecision' must eventually come to an end when you feel that the job can no longer be kept open. At this stage you must inform the sick employee without delay.

Dealing with short-term sickness

There are several steps that may be taken to control the level of sickness absence:

- have an informal talk with the employee to see if any special help is required
- you may wish to obtain an independent medical opinion on any employee who has frequent sickness absences
- try to ensure that you have a proper procedure on the provision of medical certificates and that all your staff understand and follow this policy, e.g. notification of sickness should be made as early as possible on the first day of sickness
- where necessary the employee may need to be told that the level of sick absence is putting the job at risk.

The statutory sick pay scheme allows you to operate a system of 'self-certification' for sickness absence of up to one week. The requirement to give a formal written statement of the reasons for absence can help to concentrate an employee's mind on this important matter.

Frequent absence may indicate general ill health which requires medical investigation and attention, and if it continues it may suggest that the employee is unable to continue to do the job. Obviously, you will wish to encourage staff to seek medical attention. Furthermore, you may need to explore whether there are personal or domestic difficulties or problems with the job itself. Particular attention needs to be paid to any pattern in frequent short absences on grounds of sickness; this may indicate that sickness is being used as a cover for other reasons and may emphasize the need for good supervision of staff.

Dealing with unauthorized absences, including lateness

Unauthorized absence, the occasional day off work, when sickness is often given as a reason or excuse, is generally known as 'absenteeism'. Lateness and poor timekeeping often reflect the same syndrome. All such absences may be disruptive, particularly because they occur without any prior warning, although ironically enough they may become so patterned that others can predict when they will occur: 'She always takes a day off sick after a bank holiday'.

Absenteeism and lateness often point to problems arising from the job itself; your employee may be reluctant to come to work because they are unhappy in the job or simply dislike work. These problems need to be closely investigated. Is the supervision of staff adequate? Are working relationships satisfactory? Is the job properly organized in terms of the quantity and quality of the work? Above all, such absenteeism must never be allowed to go unnoticed; you should always inquire into the matter without any delay.

Other action to be taken includes:

- keeping a careful check of the individual's record of absenteeism, time-keeping etc.
- insisting that the absent employee (or a member of the family or friend) should telephone the surgery before a specified time on the first day of absence (say 11 am)
- obtaining some indication of how long the employee is likely to be away which will help you to cope with the absence; but you may wish to require your employee to ring before a specified time on each day of absence
- ensuring that you have an informal talk with the employee on the day immediately after the period of absence
- watching closely any absences that are next to holidays and looking for other obvious patterns

• looking at the working environment. Could this be contributing to absenteeism?

Continued absences of this type may well lead to disciplinary action which eventually ends in dismissal. The disciplinary procedures that you should follow are outlined in Chapter 10.

Taking a fair, firm and sympathetic approach

You need to be fair, firm and sympathetic when handling the many varied and often difficult problems that lead to absences from work. To ensure fairness, your procedures should be applied with consistency and your employees should be aware of these. To be firm in your approach to absence, you must never hesitate to act if you have good grounds for believing that sickness is being used as an excuse for indefensible absences. Sympathy is particularly necessary when dealing with long-term sickness and special domestic or travelling difficulties. Much goodwill may be generated by giving staff authorized time off to meet occasional special needs, e.g. the illness of a child or dependent relative, a family bereavement or specific religious observances of minority groups.

10 Disciplinary action and dismissal: fair or unfair?

Where to obtain advice and assistance

BMA members should contact their local BMA office. Local ACAS offices can also provide advice.

At the time of writing it seems likely that the Government will reduce from two years to one year the qualifying length of service for protection against unfair dismissal.

Common anxieties

There is no better point to start from than the anxieties often expressed by GPs and practice managers. First, some believe that the plethora of employment law has so tied their hands that it is not only difficult but virtually impossible to sack an employee. Second, others are so reluctant to contemplate dismissal, even when it is clearly necessary, that they compound their problems by delay and a failure to follow a proper procedure. Indeed, some are so reticent that they are unwilling to dismiss a newly recruited employee who (even after adequate training and supervision) is quite unsuited to the job. Reluctance to dismiss may be associated with a failure to give proper notice of the dismissal and to follow the required procedure. These omissions almost always create greater difficulties and may so easily lead to a successful claim for compensation for unfair dismissal. Other problems arise if you try to use redundancy as the grounds for dismissal when the actual reasons are to do with misconduct or inability to do the job.

Sometimes GPs fail to consult their partners before taking action, even though the decision should be taken (or at the very least confirmed) by the partnership as a whole. A more unusual (almost bizarre) problem occurs when a practice tries to dismiss someone who is not even their employee; the most common example is an attempted dismissal of a health authority employee attached to a practice.

The content and quantity of work is always changing; your employees change through normal wastage and their own domestic circumstances, health and capabilities will also alter. More generally, there will be changes in the way in which a practice is run – practices may combine or divide, premises may be acquired or closed and new work may be taken on. All these changes may lead to a position where an employee is either unwilling to do the work that is required or incapable of doing it.

The need for change and for your employees to accept and adapt to it inevitably creates many 'grey areas' that do not seem to fit easily into the formalities of the unfair dismissal legislation. In Chapters 7 and 9 especially, I discuss ways of handling this continual process of change and adaptation. The crucial guiding principle is that you should ensure that staff are aware that change is an inevitable feature of the practice and that they should be willing to accept this and be capable of adapting to it. If they fall short in either of these respects then the procedures outlined below may have to be applied.

What is dismissal?

Hopefully, in most circumstances it should be clear to both employee and employer that a dismissal has taken place. But it should be noted that a dismissal may also occur when:

- an employee's fixed term contract expires and is not renewed
- an employer does not allow an employee who has qualified for reinstatement to return to work after pregnancy or childbirth
- an employee resigns for reasons that relate to certain conduct by the employer – this is known as 'constructive dismissal'

- an employer does not make their intentions clear, e.g. if the language or expression is unclear. Although a dismissal may not be intended, certain phrases, such as 'You know what you can do', may be reasonably interpreted in practice as notice of dismissal.

Fair reasons for dismissal

There are several aspects to any dismissal that determine whether it is fair or unfair:

- is the reason for the dismissal valid?
- has the employer acted reasonably in treating that reason as sufficient grounds for dismissing the employee?
- is the procedure followed by the employer fair?

The legislation refers to five specific types of reason that may justify dismissal.

1 *Conduct* – that is the most usual reason for dismissal and the one that is most likely to lead to a complaint of unfair dismissal.
2 *Capability* – the employee cannot satisfactorily do the job. Additional problems that may arise when illness has led to an employee being unable to do the job are discussed below.
3 *Redundancy* – normally an employee has no grounds for claiming unfair dismissal if the dismissal was because of redundancy, i.e. because the employer has no work (or insufficient work) for the employee to do and is unable to provide suitable alternative work. It is not uncommon, however, for redundancy to be used improperly as an easier alternative to 'misconduct' or 'incapacity' to effect a dismissal.
4 A *statutory requirement* – the most obvious example is when the loss of a driving licence prevents an employee from doing the job and there is no suitable alternative job available.
5 *Some other substantial reason* – this may sound like a catch-all option, but in fact it only applies to the specific and important range of circumstances described below.

Misconduct

If you dismiss a member of your staff on grounds of misconduct this will usually be the final stage of your disciplinary procedure. When contemplating or taking this action you need to consider the following points.

- Did your employee know an offence was being committed? Your disciplinary rules should be sensible and clear and your staff should be aware of them. It is essential that they should know of any conduct that constitutes gross misconduct because this could result in suspension from work on full pay, pending an investigation that may precede summary dismissal, i.e. without notice. Obviously anything you label as gross misconduct must be serious enough to warrant summary dismissal. For general practice staff a serious breach of confidentiality, an act of theft or an abuse of drugs are examples of gross misconduct. These examples may not be comprehensive. It is advisable to give examples of these in the employment contract, pointing out that the list is not comprehensive.
- It is quite unreasonable for someone to be dismissed for a first offence, except where there has been gross misconduct. If you are considering dismissal your employee should have been warned on a previous occasion when misconduct occurred that a further offence might lead to dismissal. It is advisable to give written warnings to an employee in line with the Advisory, Conciliation and Arbitration Service (ACAS) code, which is mentioned below. These may have an impact, particularly if it is made clear that it is a final written warning and that a further repetition will lead to dismissal. You may wish to ask your employee to confirm in writing receipt of your letter. It is certainly advisable to keep a written record of all warnings, not only for your own use but also as evidence if you should be faced with an industrial tribunal hearing. (It is normal for warnings to be kept 'on record' for only a specified period – say, six months for a verbal warning and 12 months for a written warning.)
- You must investigate all the facts of the case thoroughly, particularly if it is likely to lead to summary dismissal.
- Finally, for your procedures to be reasonable your employee should have an opportunity to put their side of the case, and to appeal against an adverse finding and decision. There might be an acceptable explanation for the behaviour.

ACAS has produced a code on disciplinary practice and procedures, and industrial tribunals have to take this into account when deciding whether a dismissal is fair or unfair. It is recognized that the small employer cannot be expected to follow this code to the letter. If your approach to a dismissal takes account of the issues discussed above, the main points of the ACAS code should have been covered.

Inability to do the job

There are various grounds on which an employee might be considered unable to do the job – ill health, lack of skill or qualifications, poor standard of performance.

Before you contemplate dismissing on grounds of inability you should consider the following:

- have you provided adequate training, including guidance on how the work should be done and the standards you expect?
- has your employee been properly supervised? Have you provided regular opportunities to discuss and review progress?
- was your employee told of any shortcomings as soon as these became evident? Has there been an opportunity to improve? (It is important not to allow matters to drift on)
- is the employee in the right job? If not, within the limited opportunities available could the employee be offered something more suitable?
- have you given a final warning, stating that if there is no improvement the employee will be dismissed?

More difficult problems arise when employees are absent through ill health (*see* Chapter 9). An employer with few employees may find it hard to cope with frequent or prolonged absences. The employer may be unable to keep the job open indefinitely.

Redundancy

Fortunately, redundancy is still quite rare in general practice but its frequency is increasing. Although it may be fair to dismiss an employee on these grounds because you need fewer people to do the work, you must be in a position to show that your method of selecting who should go was fair. This is vital. You should decide on the criteria of selection, e.g. length of service, skill, an objective assessment of work performance, attendance, disciplinary warnings or some combination of these. You should then consider whether you could provide another job for the person instead of redundancy. Finally, if redundancy is the only option you should give as much warning as possible, and consult those employees affected to see if their help and suggestions could avoid a redundancy.

Legal impediments to continued employment

An employee may be fairly dismissed if continued employment would result in a breach of the law. The obvious example is when someone who is employed to drive loses their licence. Nevertheless, even though this case may seem straightforward it is still necessary to show that you have acted reasonably. In particular, you would need to consider whether driving was essential to the job and whether alternative work could be available, albeit on a short-term basis, until the licence is restored.

Other substantial reasons

There are grounds for dismissal not covered by the headings above. It is difficult to specify these with precision but industrial tribunals have accepted the following as 'some other substantial reason' for fair dismissal:

- difficult relationships with other staff
- changes of duties or conditions that were not acceptable to the employee (*see* Chapter 7)
- false information (which has importance) on an application form
- reorganization of a business
- when a temporary replacement for another employee, e.g. during maternity leave, is no longer required.

In all these circumstances you should ensure that the dismissal is carried out in a reasonable manner, giving a proper explanation and due warning. Your reasons for the dismissal should be put in writing, and you should make provision in your disciplinary procedure for your employee to appeal against the decision.

Who may not complain of unfair dismissal

The main circumstances in which someone cannot complain of unfair dismissal are as follows.

- In the case of anyone who is not an employee, e.g. an independent contractor. There have been recent industrial tribunal cases where GPs themselves have been able to lodge successful claims for unfair dismissal (following the termination of a partnership) because the contractual agreement between the partners did not meet the criteria of a partnership as defined in the law of partnership. In such circumstances the consequences may be more far reaching and serious than just the risk of a successful claim for compensation on the grounds of unfair dismissal.

- Employees who have not completed two years' continuous employment by the date on which dismissal takes place unless the dismissal is for reasons which are inadmissable (this two year qualifying period is currently being challenged on the grounds that it unfairly discriminates against women – women take more career breaks and work for shorter periods, moving in and out of jobs more quickly than men).
- Employees who have already reached the normal retiring age for their employment or, if there is no normal retiring age, both men and women who have reached age 65.

Unfair dismissal and retiring age

There are several key principles relating to retiring age which affect an individual employee's right to complain of unfair dismissal:

- if the normal retiring age is the same for men and women no one may complain of unfair dismissal after that age, whatever it may be
- if there is no normal retiring age, anyone under age 65 may complain of unfair dismissal
- if the normal retiring age is discriminatory, e.g. 60 for women and 62 for men, anyone under age 65 may complain of unfair dismissal.

Normal retiring age is ascertained from the reasonable expectations of employees and may differ from contractual retiring age. It may also vary between posts and grades.

At the time of writing an industrial tribunal has held that rules which deny over-65s the right to claim unfair dismissal or redundancy breach European sex equality law. The tribunal decided that the rules were discriminatory because more men than women want to work after 65. Although tribunal rulings do not set a precedent, if the case is subsequently upheld on appeal it will open up the way for both men and women over age 65 to claim employment protection rights.

Unfair dismissal in perspective

It should be the aim of any employer to act in a fair and reasonable way in all dealings with staff. This is in the interests of good management and employment legislation is designed to encourage and support it.

Note these three features of the legislation:

- an employee cannot normally bring an unfair dismissal claim to an industrial tribunal until he or she has been with you for two years. (Unless, of course, it is claimed that the dismissal was on inadmissible grounds, e.g. pregnancy and childbirth)
- industrial tribunals must take into account the size and administrative resources of the employer when considering whether a dismissal is fair. This is to reduce the burden on small employers
- although rare in general practice, any dismissal based on discrimination against trade union activities or concerning action against anyone who has made a claim of sexual, racial or disability discrimination or discrimination on grounds of pregnancy or childbirth will be judged automatically unfair.

A tribunal hearing can be a most harrowing experience and the work required to prepare your defence and attend the hearings is both costly and time consuming to you and the practice. Thus, it is advisable to take some simple precautionary steps, particularly since these may also help you to manage the practice more effectively.

Preventative measures

Dismissal should be a rare event if you have already followed the steps below, which have already been described in Chapters 1, 3 and 7.

- Make sure that your selection procedures are adequate so that you find the right person to fill your vacancy.
- Relations with a new employee should be put on a proper footing from the outset. You are legally obliged to issue a written statement of the main terms and conditions of employment within two calendar months of the employee starting work. This statement should specify any disciplinary rules (or refer to another document containing these) and state to whom the employee should go if dissatisfied with any disciplinary decision or if they have a grievance about the job. The importance of

having adequate disciplinary and grievance procedures has been emphasized in Chapter 3.

- Try to ensure that your training arrangements are satisfactory. It is
important to act without delay if the standard of work falls below what
you require. Difficult and almost intractable problems may arise if you
allow unsatisfactory working practices to persist simply because you are
reluctant to take corrective action. Your employee will assume acceptance of unsatisfactory performance if no action is required to improve it.
- Written records are important. You should keep notes of any disciplinary
warnings (oral or written) since these may be required as evidence if your
actions ultimately lead to dismissal and a subsequent tribunal hearing.

If these steps are followed you are unlikely to face problems over dismissal. Nevertheless, even the most conscientious employer may have to consider a dismissal. Should this happen, it cannot be emphasized too often
that *there is normally a two year qualifying period before a claim for
unfair dismissal may be made.* This should provide ample time for you to
assess someone's capabilities. A new employee will serve a specified pro-
bationary period, but you have up to two years to monitor performance
before most statutory rights are acquired. Your employee should be given
the chance to improve both before and after the two year qualifying period.

As I have stated, unfair dismissal is a rare occurrence. Indeed, when it
does happen it is often a consequence of an ill-considered approach to the
necessary disciplinary action that must precede dismissal. This in turn usually arises from a reluctance to act decisively (but reasonably) when this is
necessary. Indeed, it has often been the practice's kindness and unwill-
ingness to upset an employee which has subsequently led to serious legal
difficulties and even a tribunal hearing. Preventative action is crucial, not
only because it is a necessary part of good management but also because
it will avoid the trauma of a claim of unfair dismissal.

Remember that your handling of any dismissal has both 'procedural'
and 'substantive' aspects. It is necessary to show that your approach to it
has been fair and reasonable and that the reasons for the dismissal are
reasonable, and therefore defensible, if you should be required to justify
your actions.

Lastly, if you have the misfortune to be the subject of an industrial
tribunal application (and hearing) you should seek advice from your local
BMA office without delay. Whether you win or lose the case, it is advisable to consider whether any lessons may be learnt from the episode. Was
your selection procedure lacking in some respect? Is your disciplinary
procedure effective, especially your arrangements to give an early warning
of unsatisfactory performance or behaviour?

11 Race and sex discrimination

Extent of antidiscrimination law • Sexual harassment • Points to watch

Where to obtain advice and assistance

BMA members should contact their local BMA office. Local ACAS offices can also provide advice. Further information can be obtained from the following:

- on sex discrimination: Equal Opportunities Commission, Overseas House, Quay Street, Manchester M3 3HN. Tel: 0161 833 9244
- on race discrimination: Commission for Racial Equality, Elliot House, 10–12 Allington Street, London SW1E 5EH. Tel: 0171 828 7022.

Disability discrimination, an important new area of legislation, is discussed in Chapter 12.

Few practices will have experienced any difficulties with the race and sex discrimination laws. Indeed, for any employer, avoiding discrimination per se is good management. It may seem unlikely that an employer with only a handful of staff (most of whom are already women) could be affected in any way. Both the Race Relations Act and the Sex Discrimination Act apply to all employers, irrespective of the size of their undertakings.

But there is a growing awareness of these antidiscrimination laws, heightened by the efforts of various organizations (including local councils and voluntary agencies) to inform people of their rights and to encourage and assist them in pursuing these. Influential public bodies, including the

Commission for Racial Equality, the Equal Opportunities Commission and local community relations councils, have been particularly active in this sphere. It is therefore more likely than ever that an unsuccessful applicant for a vacancy in your practice (or someone unknown to you who has not even applied for the vacancy) could seek redress on the grounds that your recruitment and selection procedures were discriminatory.

Fortunately, employers can greatly reduce any risk of an unjustifiable claim of discrimination by taking a few essential precautionary steps. Any claim of discrimination incurs the time and costs of attending an industrial tribunal hearing. If the claim is successful there are the additional costs of the compensatory award. Irrespective of its outcome, the claim will lead to unwelcome local publicity.

Extent of antidiscrimination law

Two areas where legislation requires employers to act (and to be able to show that they have acted) in a manner that is not discriminatory are:

- on the grounds of sex (including equal pay) and marital status
- on the grounds of colour, race, nationality (including citizenship) or ethnic or national origins.

If your recruitment and selection procedures, together with your employment practices, are properly conducted no difficulties should arise. The sex discrimination legislation was primarily intended to raise the opportunities and status of women in employment; however, men do have equal rights under this Act.

Fortunately, the scope and structure of both the sex and racial discrimination law are similar. Both include two types of discrimination, direct and indirect, and both require employers to take essentially the same action to ensure that their behaviour is neither discriminatory in practice nor capable of being seen as such.

Direct discrimination occurs when a person treats another person less favourably on grounds of race (or sex or both) than they treat (or would treat) someone else. It is not necessary to show that the person openly expressed an intention to discriminate: it is possible in many instances to infer that the motive was discriminatory in the light of the circumstances of their actions.

Indirect discrimination occurs when the treatment may be equal in a formal sense as between different racial groups or between persons of different sex but is discriminatory in its effect on one sex or particular racial group, e.g. the unnecessary stipulation that a cleaner should have certain educational qualifications.

When assessing whether or not an employer has acted in an indirectly discriminatory manner an industrial tribunal is required to consider whether their actions, although formally applied in a non-discriminatory manner, have the effect of being discriminatory. In the area of racial discrimination, indirect discrimination would have occurred in filling a vacancy if the following consequences occurred. The employer imposed some condition which any applicant for the vacancy must fulfil. Although this condition is applied equally to everyone irrespective of racial group, its effect is to debar persons of a particular racial group from either applying or successfully competing for the job. In these circumstances such action may provide a basis for a claim of indirect discrimination. In particular, the tribunal will consider whether the proportion of persons able to satisfy the condition in the complainant's racial group is considerably smaller than the proportion outside that group who can comply with it. If it can then be shown that the condition cannot be justified in terms of what is required for the job, indirect racial discrimination will have occurred. A similar approach is applied when assessing whether any employer's behaviour is indirectly discriminatory on grounds of sex.

There are three areas where it is unlawful to discriminate on grounds of race or sex when recruiting staff.

• In the arrangements you make for deciding who should be offered the job, e.g. in the instructions you give to an employment agency or in the way in which the job is advertised. (In practice an employment agency or newspaper should ensure that your vacancy is neither advertised nor handled in a way which is discriminatory on grounds of race or sex.) The person claiming that they have been discriminated against does not need to have applied for the job to be eligible to make a complaint about these arrangements.
• In relation to any terms offered, e.g. pay or holidays.
• By refusing or deliberately omitting to offer a person employment, e.g. by rejecting an application or by deliberately avoiding consideration of an application.

It is also unlawful for employers to discriminate on grounds of sex or race in the opportunities they provide for their employees for promotion or training or any other benefits, facilities or services. It is especially important to ensure that your procedures for promotion are fair, since this is where discrimination can easily creep in.

Box 11.1

Although not related to employment as such, it should be noted that it is unlawful for any partnership to discriminate on grounds of race or sex in the arrangements it makes for the selection of new partners, in affording a partner access to benefits, facilities or services, in opportunities for training, in dismissing a partner or in treating the partner unfavourably in any other way. These provisions also apply to persons proposing to form themselves into a partnership. (Sex discrimination legislation applies to partnerships with two or more partners, whereas race discrimination legislation applies where there are five or more partners.)

Sexual harassment

For some time the legal consequences of sexual harassment were unclear: the 1975 Sex Discrimination Act does not specifically cover harassment. However, the Act does provide that a person discriminates against a woman if 'on the grounds of sex he treats her less favourably than he treats or would treat a man', resulting in the complainant suffering a detriment, i.e. dismissal, denial of job-related benefits or 'any other detriment'.

The courts have interpreted this as including within the definition of 'treatment' conditions in the work environment. In a key case in 1986 a judge declared 'Sexual harassment is particularly degrading and is not acceptable' and 'It must have been the intention of Parliament to include such treatment within the sex discrimination legislation'. Thus, if sexual harassment is proved the remedies include a declaration that discrimination has occurred, an award of compensation (including a separate award for injury to feelings) and a recommendation that the employer take action 'to obviate or reduce the adverse effect on the complainant'.

The seriousness with which the law treats sexual harassment is reflected in the level of compensation awarded. There is no upper limit to the amount that may be awarded, and there have been several well-publicized cases where employers have paid out six figure sums.

Employers who commit or permit acts of sexual harassment may also be held to breach the contractual terms relating to mutual trust and confidence, entitling employees to resign and treat themselves as constructively dismissed. (*See* Box 11.2 for a list of actions that may constitute sexual harassment.)

Box 11.2: Actions that may constitute sexual harassment

- Unwanted physical contact such as unnecessary touching, patting or pinching of another employee's body
- Demands for sexual favours in return for promotion
- Unwelcome sexual advances or propositions
- Continued suggestions for social activity outside the workplace after it has been made clear that such suggestions are unwelcome
- Offensive flirtations
- Suggestive remarks, innuendos or lewd comments
- Display of sexually suggestive pin-ups or calendars
- Leering or eyeing up a person's body
- Derogatory remarks which are gender related
- Sexual assault
- Offensive comments about appearance or dress that are gender related
- Sexist or patronizing behaviour

Points to watch

The most important matter on which you may need to concentrate is the arrangements you make for selecting and recruiting staff. The more informal your methods, the greater the risk of being accused of discrimination, particularly on grounds of race. An approach to recruitment based on an informal 'by word of mouth' method may not only have unforeseen dangers of its own (see Chapter 1) but can easily leave you open to a claim (even from someone unknown to you who has not even applied for the vacancy) that your selection procedure is discriminatory. It is wise to retain the notes you make at the time of the interview.

High local levels of unemployment, together with changes in attitudes, may lead to more men applying for receptionist and secretarial posts – work which has been seen as a traditional preserve of women. Applications from men need to be considered on the same basis as those for women.

There are genuine occupational qualifications that allow some jobs to be excluded from the sex discrimination law but it is most unlikely that many (if any) posts in general practice would satisfy these. The Sex Discrimination Act removed the legal barriers to men becoming midwives.

Any individual who considers that they are a victim of discriminatory action may institute proceedings in an industrial tribunal if the action complained of is in the employment field. Few problems are likely to arise in general practice, but there is growing public awareness of this legislation. The sex and race discrimination laws are intended to encourage and reinforce good employment practices. It is these good practices that are important and this legislation should not be approached from the standpoint of how to meet its basic statutory requirements.

12 Disability discrimination

Defining disability • Discrimination in employment • An employer's duty to make 'adjustments' • Pensions • Liabilities under the Act

Where to obtain advice and assistance

BMA members should contact their local BMA office. Local ACAS offices are also able to advise. Copies of the various guidance documents are available from the Education and Employment Department free of charge.

Guidance on matters to be taken into account in determining questions relating to the definition of disability, Departments for Education and Employment and Social Security (or in Northern Ireland, the Departments of Economic Development and Health and Social Services), available from HMSO.

Code of Practice for the elimination of discrimination in the field of employment against disabled persons or persons who have had a disability, Department for Education and Employment (or in Northern Ireland, the Department of Economic Development), available from HMSO.

The 1995 Disability Discrimination Act means that any practice with 20 or more employees must not discriminate against disabled persons in relation to recruitment, selection, promotion and dismissal, by failing to make what are quaintly termed 'reasonable adjustments' to working arrangements or physical features at the workplace. Disability discrimination is defined as treating a disabled person less favourably than others.

If a tribunal upholds a complaint of discrimination, it may order un-limited compensation. However, until industrial tribunals have made a sufficient number of decisions, it is difficult to assess the impact of this legislation. All practices with more than 20 employees should review their policy towards employing disabled persons, particularly their recruitment, selection and promotion procedures.

Although this chapter only addresses the employment issues arising from the Act as these affect general practice, it should be noted that the Act also applies to the provision of services. Service providers (which include GPs) are required not to discriminate against disabled persons by refusing to provide goods, facilities and services or by providing them at a lower standard, in a worse manner or on worse terms than would be offered to other members of the public.

Other key features of the legislation are that:

- it applies to prospective and current employees discriminated against because of disability
- rights are acquired immediately with no qualifying periods of employment
- there are no age limits
- there are no restrictions for part-timers
- partners (as partners, but not as employers) are exempted (unlike sex and race discrimination legislation)
- compensation which is unlimited may include an amount specifically awarded for hurt feelings.

Defining disability

The definition of disability is somewhat complex. In brief, someone has a disability if they have a physical or mental impairment which has a long-term and substantive adverse effect on their ability to carry out normal day-to-day activities. Certain conditions are precluded from being treated as a disability. Government guidance on the definition must be taken into account by tribunals when considering whether a person can bring a complaint.

A disability may arise from a physical or mental impairment, including sensory impairments such as those affecting sight or hearing.

- *Mental illness.* A mental impairment is covered only if recognized by a respected body of medical opinion; any illness mentioned in publications such as the World Health Organisation's *International Classification of Diseases* is likely to be included.
- *Drug addiction.* Addiction to alcohol, nicotine or any other substance is not an impairment unless it originally resulted from taking drugs or

other medical treatment. However, a person can develop an impairment because of drug addiction which may amount to a recognized disability even if the addiction itself does not qualify, e.g. liver disease caused by alcoholism.

- *Personality disorders*. Some personality disorders are not 'impairments', e.g. moods, mild eccentricities, pyromania, kleptomania, tendency to physical or sexual abuse, exhibitionism and voyeurism.

Substantial adverse effect

To be a disability, an impairment must substantially affect someone's ability to carry out normal day-to-day activities, which include mobility and manual dexterity. And for the effect to be 'substantial' it must be more than minor or trivial.

The aim is to encapsulate the normal meaning of 'disability' as a limitation going well beyond differences in ability which normally exist among people. When assessing the effect, both the time taken to carry out the activity and how it is carried out should be taken into account. Furthermore, both direct and indirect effects of an impairment should be assessed, e.g. someone may have been given medical advice to limit their activity or may be limited in carrying out an activity by the pain or fatigue associated with it.

- *Cumulative effects*. It is an impairment's overall effect that is decisive. Even if a person's impairment only marginally affects their ability to carry out each day-to-day activity taken separately, there may be a substantial cumulative effect on their ability to carry out those activities overall. It may also be necessary to assess the cumulative effect of more than one impairment, e.g. a person's ability may be substantially impaired by the combined effect of both a minor disablement on their co-ordination and a minor leg injury affecting mobility.
- *Surrounding circumstances*. The effect of a person's impairment may vary according to the time of day or night, and whether or not the person is tired or stressed. When assessing whether the impairment is substantial, the impact of these factors should be taken into account.
- *Managing impairment*. Account should also be taken of the extent to which someone can reasonably be expected to modify their behaviour to reduce the effects of an impairment. If the person can manage the impairment such that the effect is minor, then he or she no longer meets the definition of disability, whether or not they actually take those steps. However, it may be necessary to take account of the possibility that a person's ability to manage their impairment may be affected by the

surrounding circumstances, e.g. where someone with a stutter is placed under stress. Because the legislation stipulates that the effect of a person's impairment has to be assessed without taking account of any measures being taken to treat or correct it, any action based on medical advice to manage an impairment may need to be disregarded when deciding whether the person has a disability.

- *Severe disfigurement.* This is normally regarded as having a substantial effect on someone's ability to carry out normal day-to-day activities, whether or not it actually does so. Examples include scars, birthmarks, limb or postural deformations and skin diseases. An assessment of a disfigurement may need to take account of its position on the person's body, but it should not be regarded as 'substantial' if it is a tattoo or body piercing.

Long-term effect

For someone to have a disability within the Act's definition, the adverse effect must be long term, i.e. lasting at least 12 months or likely to do so. When deciding whether it is long term, the typical length of such an effect and the person's characteristics, e.g. health and age, should be taken into account.

The effect of an impairment need not be the same throughout the 12 month period to meet the long-term criterion – its original effects may diminish or disappear but other adverse effects may continue. Provided the impairment has (or is likely to have) a substantial effect throughout a 12 month period it should be regarded as long term.

Special provision is made for conditions which are subject to remission but then recur. If such an impairment has a substantial adverse effect when it occurs, it is treated as continuing during the remission period if it is likely to recur. When assessing the likelihood of a recurrence, it is necessary to take into account anything which a person might reasonably be expected to do to prevent the recurrence, e.g. avoiding substances to which they are allergic. If medical or other treatment is likely to cure an impairment so that it would be unlikely to recur without further treatment, then this should be taken into account. However, if the treatment simply delays or prevents a recurrence, which would be likely if the treatment were stopped, then the normal rule that the treatment must be disregarded applies and the effect must be regarded as likely to recur.

- *Hay fever.* One condition which is likely to recur in this way is seasonal allergic rhinitis. Because hay fever is not generally viewed as a disability, the legislation states that it should not be treated as an impairment, although it can be taken into account if it aggravates e.g. if a respiratory disorder is aggravated by hay fever, the overall effect of the two conditions can be taken into account. Even if the effect of a person's respiratory disorder is usually minor, if it is substantial when aggravated by the hay fever it may satisfy the definition of disability.

Discrimination in employment

The Act makes it unlawful for an employer to treat a person with a disability less favourably for a reason relating to it than someone to whom that reason does not or would not apply, unless it can be shown that such treatment is justified.

The Government issued a Code of Practice advising employers how to avoid discrimination. Although it is not unlawful to ignore the Code, industrial tribunals hearing complaints of disability discrimination must take account of it. The Code includes examples of how the Act operates and guidance on how to comply with it. In particular, it emphasizes that to avoid unlawful discrimination an employer should:

- *be flexible* – there may be several ways to avoid discrimination in any one situation, many of which cost little or nothing to implement
- *avoid making assumptions* – talk to each disabled person about the real effects of their disability and what help might be given. The likelihood of misunderstandings is greatly reduced if the person is involved from the start
- *consider whether expert advice is needed* – if appropriate, seek independent advice on a disabled person's capabilities and what might be done to change premises or working arrangements, especially if your discussions with your employee do not lead to a fruitful solution
- *plan ahead* – when planning changes consider the needs of possible future disabled employees and applicants. Useful improvements could be built into plans
- *promote equal opportunities* – employers who follow a good disability discrimination policy (and monitor its effectiveness) are likely to have that counted in their favour by a tribunal if a complaint is made.

Justification

The Code emphasizes that less favourable treatment of a disabled person is justified only if the reason for it is both material to the circumstances of the case and substantial. For example, turning down a disabled person for employment solely because other employees would be uncomfortable working alongside them would be unlawful and the same rule would apply if it were thought that customers would feel uncomfortable.

Pay

Pay arrangements linking reward to performance could amount to unlawful discrimination, since some disabled people's work performance may be affected by disability. This discriminatory treatment is only justified if it results from applying to a disabled person a term or practice under which an employee's pay is wholly or partly dependent on their performance, and if it applies to the whole workforce or that part of it which includes the disabled person.

An employer's duty to make 'adjustments'

Employers are required to modify those aspects of their premises or working arrangements which put disabled employees or job applicants at a substantial disadvantage. A failure to comply with this duty is unlawful discrimination unless it can be justified. Furthermore, if an employer treats a disabled person less favourably for a reason relating to their disability and has unjustifiably failed to make reasonable modifications, their discriminatory behaviour cannot normally be justified.

The Code of Practice illustrates what employers have to do and those factors determining whether it is reasonable for the employer to make modifications, e.g. the Code says that it would be reasonable for an employer to spend at least as much on an adjustment to retain a disabled person (including any retraining) as might be spent on recruiting and training a replacement.

Modifying premises

In relation to an employer's duty to make reasonable modifications to premises, the following are treated as physical features (permanent or temporary):

- any feature arising from the design or construction of a building
- any feature of an approach to, exit from or access to a building
- any fixtures, fittings, furnishings, furniture, equipment or materials in or on the premises
- any other physical element or quality of any land.

It is never reasonable for an employer to take steps which would remove any physical feature from their premises which was originally adopted in order to satisfy the requirements of building regulations dealing with access and facilities for disabled people.

- *Restrictions in mortgages and covenants.* An employer may be under a binding obligation, such as a condition in a mortgage or a restrictive covenant, to obtain someone else's consent before altering the premises. In these circumstances, it is usually reasonable for the employer to seek that consent, except if this involves applying to a court or tribunal.
- *Leases.* The Act makes special provision for employers who occupy leasehold premises by overriding a restrictive lease to enable them to alter them, provided they apply in writing for the landlord's consent, which must not be unreasonably withheld but may be subject to reasonable conditions.

An employer cannot argue that they have been prevented from making reasonable alterations by a lease, unless they have applied for consent to do so. On the other hand, it is not reasonable for an employer to have to act contrary to the lease if:

- they have applied to the landlord for consent
- the landlord has withheld consent
  and
- the employer has informed the disabled person that the landlord has withheld consent.

If the employer has taken these steps, they are not liable for failing to make the changes but the landlord may be. If a discrimination complaint arises either the complainant or the employer can ask the tribunal to join the landlord as a part of the proceedings. The tribunal will then decide whether the landlord unreasonably refused consent or imposed unreasonable conditions. If they have, the tribunal may authorize the employer to make the alterations, and may order the landlord to pay compensation.

Pensions

Although employers are under an obligation not to discriminate against disabled people in relation to occupational pensions, the duty to make 'reasonable adjustments' does not apply to pension benefits. Furthermore, discrimination is also lawful if a person's disability and prognosis mean that the cost of providing benefits for them in relation to termination of service, retirement, old age, death, accident, injury, sickness or invalidity is likely to be substantially greater than it would be for a comparable person without that disability. In these circumstances, the employer is justified in treating the disabled person less favourably in relation to eligibility conditions for, or the amount of, these benefits. However, this less favourable treatment may only be possible when a disabled person is considered for admission to the scheme; once a member, a disabled person can only be treated less favourably for a reason relating to that disability if the terms on which they were admitted allow for this.

Even if a disabled person is not eligible to receive the same type or amount of benefits as other employees, the employer is justified in requiring them to pay the same rate of contribution as it requires from other employees.

Liabilities under the Act

The Act makes employers legally responsible for disability discrimination committed by employees, unless they can show that they took 'such steps as were reasonably practicable' to prevent it. An important part of the Code of Practice deals with establishing management systems to avoid discrimination, emphasizing the need to tell employees about policies on employment of disabled people and to provide training and guidance on its implementation.

An employer is only released from making a reasonable 'adjustment' if they do not know, and could not reasonably be expected to know, that someone has a disability. However, the employer must therefore do all they can reasonably be expected to do to find out whether or not this is the case. On the other hand, once an employer knows about a person's disability, they may need to maintain its confidentiality and the Code advises on how to reconcile confidentiality with making reasonable 'adjustments'.

13 Part-time staff

Most practices employ a high proportion of part-time staff. When a full-time post becomes vacant there may be a choice between finding a full-time replacement, employing two or more part-time staff or not filling the vacancy. The choice probably depends on the availability of suitable staff, on whether existing full-time staff are willing to work longer hours or simply on the traditions of the practice organization. Only the practice can decide which staffing arrangements are best suited to its particular needs. Some factors that may need to be taken into account when reaching a decision are the costs and benefits of employing either whole-time or part-time employees, and the legal, financial and administrative implications of these employment arrangements.

Advantages and disadvantages

Some advantages of employing part-time staff are:

- staffing levels can be matched more easily with predictable levels of workload. Part-timers can provide additional cover during busy periods and allow staffing levels to be cut during slack periods, thus reducing total staff costs

- most surgery staff are often reluctant to take sick leave. But there is reputedly a lower rate of absenteeism among part-time staff; domestic commitments and appointments can be arranged during the employee's own time
- the use of part-time staff can reduce the need for additional payments to full-time staff for overtime or unsocial hours
- the surgery may be more easily run continuously with part-time staff by providing cover for meal breaks and the early morning and evening shifts
- there is the option of job sharing which is growing in popularity. This arrangement enables two people to agree to share the responsibilities of a single full-time job and the pay and benefits in proportion to the hours each works.

Disadvantages of employing part-time staff may include:

- problems of continuity may still arise if there is difficulty in matching morning, afternoon and evening shifts
- the purely administrative costs of employing two part-timers are often higher than those of one full-time employee
- the rate of turnover, i.e. resignation, among part-timers is often higher; their commitment to the employer may be weaker and their earnings may not be so important in relation to the total family income
- they may be less committed to the practice than full-time staff and thus may be less willing to acquire new skills and to be flexible in their working arrangements.

Employment rights

The part-time employee no longer has fewer rights of employment protection than their full-time counterpart.

Administering part-time contracts

If the part-time employee has more than one part-time job income tax may be deducted by either the principal employer or by two or more employers. The tax office will make the necessary arrangements by allotting an appropriate coding.

Table 13.1: Employment rights of part-timers

Employment rights of part-timers	Qualifying length of service for all employees		
Not to be dismissed or discriminated against on grounds of pregnancy, maternity, marital status, sex, colour, race, nationality, ethnic and national origins, and disability	No threshold – from first day of employment		
Unfair dismissal protection	2 years	*5 years	** no right
Statutory redundancy payments	2 years	*5 years	** no right
Written statement of employment particulars – for example, a contract of employment	2 years	*5 years	** no right
Itemized pay statement	No threshold – from first day of employment		** no right
Return to work after 14 weeks' maternity leave	No threshold – from first day of employment		
Return to work after 40 weeks of maternity leave	2 years	*5 years	** no right
Written statement of reasons for dismissal	2 years	*5 years	** no right
Time off for trade union duties and activities	No threshold – from first day of employment	*5 years	** no right
Time off for public duties	No threshold – from first day of employment	*5 years	** no right
Time off to look for work or arrange training in a redundancy situation	2 years		
Guaranteed payments	1 month	*5 years	** no right
Notice of dismissal	1 month	*5 years	** no right
Payment on medical suspension	1 month	*5 years	** no right

* previous threshold for employees working 8–16 hours
** previous threshold for employees working fewer than 8 hours

Note: At the time of writing it seems likely that the Government will reduce the qualifying length of service from two years to one year.

For National Insurance, the lower earnings limit is reviewed annually. If an employee earns less than this neither the employer nor the employee pays NI contributions on the employee's earnings. If, however, the employee earns an amount greater than or equal to this, employer and employee pay contributions on the whole of the employee's earnings. Savings may be made if a pattern of hours is agreed so that total pay does not exceed the lower earnings limit.

Married women who are part-time employees (and full-time employees) earning above the lower earnings limit may be paying either full rate class 1 NI contributions or the lower rate married women's contributions. But since May 1977, the option of paying a married women's rate of contribution has been phased out. Married women who paid the lower rate before May 1977 may continue to do so. If a married woman has been away from employment for two complete tax years she must pay the full rate of contributions when she returns to work.

Hours of work and pay

The hours of work of part-time staff vary greatly according to the needs of the practice. Some part-timers may be employed two or three hours a day to cover the midday meal break or the busy periods during the morning, afternoon or evening surgery. Other arrangements may require only a couple of hours a day two or three days a week or even a few hours on alternate weeks.

Should part-time staff be paid overtime rates? There are different views of what constitutes 'overtime' for such staff:

- any work in excess of a full-time working week, e.g. beyond 40 hours a week
- any work in excess of daily full-time hours, e.g. beyond eight hours a day
- any work after normal business hours, e.g. working well beyond the end of evening surgery
- any work in excess of the contracted part-time hours.

In practice most employers pay overtime rates to part-timers only when they work beyond the full-time working week. And this will in turn depend on whether any full-time staff are paid overtime rates. The danger of paying part-timers overtime rates for time worked in excess of their part-time hours is that full-time staff may see it as being unfair to them, and they may prefer to opt for part-time contracts so that they benefit from these premium rates. One arrangement may be to decide to fix the part-time rates as a percentage of the full-time rate – say, 80% – and then to pay an overtime premium rate to part-time staff, which brings them into line with the basic full-time hourly rate.

Pensions

In the past part-timers rarely qualified for occupational pension schemes. Now the position is radically different; it is illegal to discriminate against part-timers in relation to their eligibility to join a pension scheme and they are entitled to pro-rata equivalence in respect of scheme benefits. Thus part-time practice staff enjoy the same rights in relation to the NHS pension scheme as whole-timers.

Part-timers' entitlement to state basic pensions depends on their NI contribution record. A married woman over age 60 can only qualify in her own right if she has paid full rate NI contributions for a qualifying period. If she has opted for the married woman's reduced rate of NI contribution she only qualifies for the lower rate of pension on her husband's contributions.

Maternity arrangements

Maternity leave

Every woman, irrespective of her length of service, has a right to 14 weeks' maternity leave, and not to be dismissed on grounds of pregnancy or childbirth. In addition, subject to certain qualifying conditions, a woman employee is entitled to take up to a maximum of 40 weeks' maternity leave (starting any time after the 11th week before the baby is due, together with 29 weeks after the birth). The period of leave may be extended in certain circumstances. Entitlement to 40 weeks' maternity leave depends on the employee having 104 weeks' continuous service. This service must be completed by the 11th week before the expected date of confinement.

Any woman who qualifies for maternity leave is also entitled to return either to her previous job or to other suitable work if it is not 'reasonably practicable' for her employer to offer her previous job back. But if the employer has five or fewer employees the woman cannot claim unfair dismissal if it is impracticable to take her back. After her maternity leave a woman may prefer to return to work part-time. Although there is at present no statutory legal obligation on an employer to agree to this arrangement, and it may be particularly difficult for an employer with few staff to adjust staffing to accommodate this change, there are good grounds for giving consideration to a request of this kind. It is probable that the right to return on a part-time basis could be made legally binding on employers in the future.

Statutory maternity pay

The qualifying conditions for statutory maternity pay are different from those for maternity leave. Part-time staff are eligible for statutory maternity pay if they have 26 weeks' continuous employment, normally weekly earnings of not less than the National Insurance lower limit, and give 21 days' prior notice of intended absence. Employees with two years' continuous employment are eligible for a higher rate of statutory maternity pay for the first six weeks.

Unfair dismissal

Under new legislation it is now automatically unfair to dismiss an employee because she is pregnant irrespective of length of service.

Paid time off for antenatal care

All pregnant employees have a right to take 'reasonable' paid time off to attend antenatal clinics. Except for a request for a first appointment, the employee may be asked by her employer to produce a certificate stating that she is pregnant and an appointment card showing the time of her appointment. Because this is a comparatively new statutory legal right few problems have arisen. It may be reasonable, however, for an employer to ask a part-time employee to try to arrange the appointment outside working hours.

Sick pay

Part-time employees are entitled to receive statutory sick pay from their employers. They qualify for sick pay irrespective of whether they pay full or reduced NI contributions. The employer is responsible for paying statutory sick pay for the first 28 weeks of an employee's sick leave in a tax year. After this, part-time employees still on sick leave only qualify for state sick benefit if they have paid the full NI contributions for the qualifying period.

Employees should know where they stand

In deciding what arrangements to make for your part-time staff you need to make sure that all staff know exactly where they stand. The arrangements applying to part-timers, i.e. their pay, holidays, sick leave and hours of work, should be spelt out in an employment contract.

Finally, because general practice employs such a very high proportion of part-timers, recent changes to the law which effectively prohibit any form of discrimination against part-timers and gives part-timers the same statutory employment rights as their whole-time equivalents are of particular significance to practice managers and GPs.

14 Health and safety at work

Practices' duties to their staff • Duties to other users of the premises • Enforcement • COSHH regulations • New health and safety regulations • General health and safety management • Provision and use of work equipment • Manual handling • Health, safety and welfare at work • Personal protective equipment • VDU health and safety regulations

Where to obtain advice and assistance

Your local HSE office should be able to advise on most matters. BMA members who find themselves in dispute about a health and safety matter should contact their local BMA office. Be wary of any self-proclaimed experts and/or consultants offering their services in this field. They could be both costly and wrong.

The Health and Safety at Work Act 1974 (HSW) laid down a new approach to occupational health, safety and welfare, and applies to virtually all premises where people are employed, including laboratories, hospitals and general practice surgeries.

The Health and Safety Executive (HSE), combining the factory inspectorate and other central government inspectorates, is responsible to the Health and Safety Commission. Local authority environmental health officers inspect premises and enforce the legislation in the non-industrial sector, and they follow guidance from the Commission. Because general practice premises are grouped with hospitals and laboratories in the category of 'health services', the HSE carries out inspections.

The Act lays down duties on employers (including the self-employed) to provide and maintain a safe place of work. It establishes powers and penalties to enforce safety laws, and its aim is to make all employers and employees aware of the need for safety at the place of work. Although much of this legislation is concerned with employers who already recognize trade unions – there is a requirement to appoint union safety representatives and establish a safety committee if requested to do so – even practices who have only a few employees and do not recognize trade unions have duties to fulfil.

Some of the most significant regulations made under the HSW Act are those relating to the control of hazardous substances (*see* p. 119 for the COSHH regulations, and a batch of others stemming from European Union directives that came into force on 1 January 1993).

Practices' duties to their staff

The most important duties in the Act are those of an employer to an employee. (Practices with staff who are employed by a health authority have other lesser duties.) The Act states: 'It shall be the duty of every employer to ensure, so far as is reasonably practicable, the health, safety and welfare at work of all his employees'. Thus, practices are required to do all that is *reasonably practicable* to ensure the safety of their employees. Any proceedings that may be taken under the Act are criminal. An employee can report a breach of the employer's statutory duty under the Act to the HSE who may bring criminal charges. Although the Act does not in itself confer a right of civil action on the employee, it does not prevent the employees, if injured, suing their employers for being in breach of their liability as an employer or for negligence under the common law.

What is reasonably practicable?

In assessing whether it was reasonably practicable for a practice to avoid a specific hazard or risk of injury, a court may well look at the cost of any preventive measures, particularly if the practice's resources are limited, and weigh this against the risk of personal injury and its likely severity.

The Act requires all equipment and systems of work to be safe and without risk to health; these include waste bins, sterilizers, photocopying machines, electric fires, electric typewriters, furniture, fire extinguishers, plugs and any other potentially hazardous equipment. Importance is attached to the maintenance and renewal of equipment; HSE inspectors are particularly concerned about the arrangements for regular servicing. Attention is also paid to the age, reliability, appropriateness and position of equipment.

Safe systems of working must be understood and used by everyone. Obvious examples include ensuring that staff do not lift heavy weights without help if there is a risk of back injury, that arrangements are made for the safe disposal of clinical waste, that care is taken in storing flammable liquids, materials (such as paper) and drugs and that the health of staff is not put at risk by the use of VDUs.

Any offences under the Medicines Act, the Poisons Act or the Misuse of Drugs Act 1971 lie outside the remit of the HSW Act. So any unauthorized access to drugs is more likely to be of interest to the Home Office than the HSE.

Misuse of drugs

Since there may be some overlap of the work of these Government bodies, brief reference should be made to the Misuse of Drugs Act 1971 and its regulations. Most practices will have encountered drug abuse in one form or another. This Act aims at restricting the availability of certain specified drugs of dependence. The following safety precautions apply to such drugs. They must be kept in a 'locked receptacle' which can be opened only by the doctor or an authorized person. This does not mean that these duties are absolved if the key of the receptacle is hidden in a drawer or some other 'secret place', since this could be the first place where an unauthorized person might search. Also, the courts do not accept a locked car as a 'locked receptacle' within the meaning of the regulations, so emergency bags, if they have to be left in cars, should also be locked.

In large dispensing practices, where substantial quantities of controlled drugs may be stored, the advice of the local crime prevention officer on appropriate security precautions should be obtained. Both the police and inspectors of the Home Office Drugs Branch are concerned with the enforcement of the Misuse of Drugs Act, and any breach is a criminal offence.

A written statement of safety policy is required

Under the HSW Act practices should provide information, training and supervision to ensure the health and safety of their staff. Specifically, unless the practice employs fewer than five staff, it must prepare a written statement of its policy 'with respect to the health and safety' of its employees and the organization and arrangements for carrying out this policy – for example, any safety rules that apply to potentially hazardous operations undertaken by medical and nursing staff – and the immediate action required by staff in respect of accidents and mishaps that might occur. The employees should be consulted about its form and content. Although it is not necessary in a small practice to give everybody a copy of this written statement, it may be advisable to do so. A practice may easily overlook a change in its legal obligation when the number of employees increases. The statement could be pinned on a notice board, but if the practice wishes to show that it has been drawn to everyone's attention it is advisable to give everyone a copy. Once the requirement to provide a written statement is established – that is, you have five or more employees – it should cover everyone working on the premises.

The statement should be simple and avoid excessive wording that may detract from its impact. But the safety rules should be as comprehensive as necessary so that both the practice and the safety inspector can ensure that these are adequate. For example, all staff should be reminded to report immediately any incident that might cause a risk to health or safety. The written statement could be included in each employee's contract of employment and could take the form shown in Box 14.1.

Box 14.1: Specimen health and safety at work policy statement

The practice's policy on health and safety at work is to provide as safe and healthy working conditions as possible and to enlist the support of its employees towards achieving this end. While the overall responsibility rests with the employer, all staff have a legal duty to take reasonable care to avoid injury to themselves or to others in their work activities and not to interfere with or misuse any clothing or equipment provided to protect health and safety. The main hazards that staff should be aware of are:

- medical instruments etc in the consulting room
- prams, bicycles etc.

Any accident to a member of the staff or a member of the public should be reported to the doctor in charge as soon as possible. You should record in writing a factual statement covering to the fullest possible extent all the circumstances of the accident at the time so that any necessary action may be taken to prevent a recurrence.

Your policy statement should also include the practice's policy on violence (see below).

Violence to staff

Because practice staff have direct contact with the public, they may be sworn at, threatened or even attacked. The HSE's definition of violence is: 'Any incident in which an employee is abused, threatened or assaulted by a member of the public in circumstances arising out of the course of his or her employment'.

Both employers and employees have an interest in reducing violence at work. For employers, violence lowers morale and undermines the image of the organization and makes it more difficult to recruit and retain staff. For employees, violence can of course cause pain, suffering and even disability or death. Physical attacks are obviously dangerous but serious or persistent verbal abuse or threats can also damage an employee's health through anxiety or stress or even be a precursor to physical attack.

All employers have a legal duty under the health and safety at work legislation to ensure, as far as reasonably practicable, that their employees are protected from assaults. The HSE suggests the following action for employers and employees to decide how to prevent violence.

- Find out if there is a problem by asking staff if they ever feel threatened or under great stress.
- Encourage staff to report all incidents so that you can build up a picture of the problem (a report form can help to show that this is what you expect). It is helpful to classify them according to place, time, type of incident and who was involved, so that you can look for common causes, areas or times of attack, and target remedies where they are most needed.
- Look at how jobs might be redesigned to reduce the risk of violence; examples of measures that have worked for some organizations include:
  - training employees to deal with aggression generally by spotting early signs and avoiding or coping with it
  - changing the layout of public waiting areas; better seating, decor, lighting and more regular information about delays have helped to stop tension building up
  - installing video cameras or alarm buttons can help to protect staff
  - using coded security locks or doors helps to keep the public out of prohibited areas.
- Your staff should be involved in making decisions about any redesign of working arrangements and in the implementation of other measures to prevent violence. A mix of measures may work best. It is important to try to reach a reasonable balance between the risks to your employees against possible side effects on the public; an atmosphere that suggests employees are worried about violence can increase its likelihood.
- Whatever measures are decided on, you should include your policy for dealing with violence in your health and safety policy statement so that all employees are aware of it. This helps your employees to cooperate with you, follow procedures properly and report any incidents. Once

you have taken steps to reduce the risk of violence, you should check how well they are working. Continue to record incidents and monitor what effect preventive methods have had.

The BMA's General Medical Services Committee has prepared its own advice (*see* Appendix A) to GPs on how to deal with violence.

Maintaining the building

The practice, 'so far as is reasonably practicable as regards any place of work under [its] control', must ensure that the building is maintained in a safe condition, without risks to health. The practice owners must provide a safe means of entrance and exit for staff. But if the health centre is under the direct control of a health authority the practice can only do what is reasonable on its part, and any blame may ultimately lie with the authority. For example, if there is loose guttering which the health authority is under a duty to maintain according to the licence between it and the practice, *so long as the practice has notified the authority of the danger, preferably in writing*, the practice would be exonerated from liability if an accident occurred. The practice should, however, also follow up the letter to check whether action was being taken by the authority. (Liability would fall on the authority under the Defective Premises Act 1972 and the HSW Act, since it is both the owner of the premises and those in control of maintenance who are responsible.) Similar considerations may arise when premises are rented from a private landlord. It may be advisable for a practice to examine the licence or lease under which the premises are held to clarify whose burden it is to maintain specific parts of the premises. The staff also have a responsibility to report any risks to health and safety.

A practice may not be exonerated of all responsibility for the safety of the premises, even if it does not own them; it may be held responsible for hazards such as highly polished and slippery floors and unsafe electrical flex. But if the practice is responsible for maintaining the premises it must be concerned with other parts, including for example, the condition of steps and stairways, floors and floor covering.

The Act also states that, as far as is reasonably practicable, the employer must provide and maintain a working environment for employees that is without risk to health, with adequate provision for their general welfare. The wording appears to apply to more than just the physical environment of the employee. Here a practice would be well advised to consider whether there is an adequate rest room, refreshment facilities and toilet and washing arrangements etc. Again, the extent to which this can be done must depend on the practice's resources.

Safety representatives and safety officers

Not all practices will have safety representatives and safety committees. These are normally appointed only where trade unions are recognized for negotiating purposes. In premises where there is more than one employer, however – for example, health centres – they will normally be required. Employee safety representatives can inspect the workplace, investigate accidents, make representations to the practice and insist on a joint safety committee being appointed. Safety representatives have the legal right to challenge an employer on all matters affecting health and safety standards in the workplace.

But the Health and Safety Commission has recommended that similar arrangements for safety committees and safety representatives should be made even if staff are not unionized. It considers that, since both the employer and employee share a statutory duty to ensure the health, safety and welfare at work of all, an employer may find it helpful if employees contribute to developing and improving health and safety procedures. The Commission has therefore recommended that in non-unionized workplaces the employer should set up a safety committee drawn from both management and staff. This is hardly practicable in a small practice, so it may be preferable to nominate a member of staff to serve as the 'safety officer' and monitor standards. The practice manager may wish to undertake this duty. The 'safety officer' should report directly to the partners who are the 'controllers' of the premises.

Duties to other users of the premises

Although the purpose of the Health and Safety at Work Act is to ensure the safety of employees, it also applies to all persons who enter the premises – staff employed by a health authority working on the premises, visitors, patients and sundry 'tradespeople' such as postal workers, window cleaners, builders and electricians. The Act imposes a duty on the practice as the 'controller' of the premises to ensure the safety of anyone who legitimately visits the premises. A health authority or a private landlord may also have a duty under the licence or lease, and may also be liable if an accident occurs.

The law requires practices to ensure, as far as is reasonably practicable, that all persons not in their employment who could be affected are not exposed to risks to their health and safety. This part of the Act links up with the civil liability of an occupier of premises under the Occupier's

Liability Act 1957. It may be assumed that the standards expected under the HSW Act are equal to the 'common duty of care' under the Occupier's Liability Act owed to all persons legitimately entering the premises. Under the civil law it is advisable for a practice to anticipate who might be directly affected and to ensure that the premises are safe. A practice would be well advised to consider whether there are any potential hazards for elderly or infirm patients.

The important differences between these duties and those to the practice's staff is that the staff should be provided with a written safety policy and be instructed and supervised on safety matters, and that quite specific arrangements should be made for their health, safety and welfare. The Act is intended to protect people at work but, almost as an afterthought, it has protected everybody who may be affected by the work.

Notifying accidents and dangerous occurrences

The regulations on notifying accidents and dangerous occurrences are relevant because they impose a statutory obligation on all employers to keep a record of accidents occurring on their premises and to notify the Health and Safety Executive of certain serious accidents. GPs are liable as 'controllers of premises' to notify the HSE of certain accidents to their staff and to anyone else who happens to be on the premises, such as patients, workmen or health authority staff.

Accidents and dangerous occurrences may be divided into three categories.

1 Notifiable accidents

These include fatal accidents (and those accidents that prove to be fatal within a year of their occurrence) and major injuries. A major injury is defined as a fracture of the skull, spine, pelvis, any bone in the leg (other than in the ankle or foot), any bone in the arm (other than in the wrist or hand), amputation of a hand or foot, the loss of sight of any eye or any other injury that results in the person injured being admitted into hospital as an inpatient for more than 24 hours, unless that person is detained only for observation.

These accidents must be reported to the HSE if they occur to anyone on the premises. There are two exceptions from the reporting requirements. In the unlikely event of a patient who is undergoing treatment in the surgery suffering an injury that is caused by the treatment the injury need not be reported. Accidents to a self-employed person working on the premises, unless he or she is under the control of another person, are also excluded from the reporting procedures.

2 Other accidents

These do not have to be reported to the HSE. They include what are known in industry as 'three day accidents'. This category applies only to the general practice's own staff, not to other health authority employees working on the premises. These accidents are notified to the HSE by the Department of Health (not by the GP) only if the employee makes a claim for industrial injury benefit.

3 Dangerous occurrences

These mostly apply to industrial premises; few are likely to happen in general practice. From the list of dangerous occurrences that have to be reported, only one type may be relevant. This is when a person is affected by the inhalation, ingestion or other absorption of any substance or lack of oxygen to an extent that it causes acute ill health requiring medical treatment. This could be caused by a defective central heating system.

Reporting accidents

GPs are responsible for reporting an accident, although in some circumstances responsibility lies with the owner of the premises. It is advisable for them to assume they are responsible for notifying the HSE, even if they do not carry responsibility for the premises.

Any notifiable accident must be directly notified to the local office of the HSE by telephone. It is advisable to keep a written record of the call, including the name of the civil servant receiving it and the details of the accident as given over the telephone. Within seven days a written report should be sent to the HSE. If an accident in Category 2 occurs the Department of Health will send an accident inquiry form to the practice.

Written records

It is a legal requirement for every employer to keep an accident book on the premises. A record must be kept of all notifiable accidents and dangerous occurrences, so that the employer can monitor these and identify any preventive action that should be taken. Failure to do so could lead to a fine of up to £5000.

Oddly enough, the self-employed person is exempt from the reporting procedure: thus GPs need not report accidents to themselves.

Building work on the premises

Serious hazards can arise when building work is in progress. The main contractor, subcontractor and their employees have the prime duty to carry out their work in a safe manner. The practice's duty as 'controller' of the premises is to ensure that staff, other employees on the premises, patients and visitors are not put at risk. If unavoidable temporary hazards are caused by building work these should be identified and their risks reduced as far as possible by providing warning notices that can be easily read by everyone using the premises. If GPs are in any doubt about their responsibilities they may seek clarification from the local HSE office.

Clearing snow

A practice may take steps to clear snow and ice from paths on the premises and from adjacent public pavements. But a good deed of this kind may well increase their liability to users of these pathways. If someone is subsequently injured on a cleared pathway the person who has cleared the snow may be held liable. Uncleared snow usually carries no liability of this kind, since it is assumed that the person walking on it will exercise due care and attention. However, in a recent court case, a vacuum cleaner engineer who hurt his back after slipping on icy steps was awarded more than £100 000 damages. The couple who had called him out had failed to salt the frozen steps at their home despite knowing he was about to arrive. The engineer suffered a chronic lumbar ligament strain and had not worked for over four years. The couple knew the steps could be a hazard in freezing conditions. Failure to put down salt or shout a warning was a breach of the common duty of care by the householder.

Duties of the staff

Although the heaviest responsibilities lie with employers, important reciprocal duties also lie with staff. This is to ensure that employers and employees cooperate to provide a safe place of work. Employees should take reasonable care for their own health and safety and those of others who may be affected by their actions and omissions. They should cooperate with their employer or any other person – such as the health and safety inspector – who has responsibilities under the Act.

All employees have these duties to fulfil, both the practice's own employees and any health authority staff. The duties on employees apply 'while at work', throughout the time when they are in the practice's employment 'but not otherwise'. What does 'but not otherwise' mean? Would an employee be liable if an accident happened during a lunch or a tea break taken on the premises? It seems likely that any activities that are reasonably incidental to the employment – that is, the sort of activity a 'reasonable' employee would indulge in – will be included, e.g. making tea in the kitchen or using the toilet or washing facilities. This is important because self-catering facilities are often hazardous but neglected.

Every employee (and indeed any other person) is under a duty not to interfere with or misuse anything provided for the purpose of health and safety. This protects appliances and arrangements to ensure people's safety, such as fire escapes, fire extinguishers and hazard warning notices. This could be extended to include interference with anything provided for welfare purposes, such as cloakroom and refreshment facilities. The extra responsibility placed upon employees by this Act is reflected in the far greater number of prosecutions against employees since it was implemented in 1975.

Enforcement

The Act covers all 'places of employment' and its inspectors therefore have the right to inspect practice premises. The HSE has divided the country into areas and each has its own team of inspectors. One group of inspectors in each area is responsible for the 'health services', which includes general practice.

Powers of the inspectors

Inspectors have a warrant of appointment that states their extensive powers and practices may ask to see this for identification purposes. Inspectors normally have the right to enter any premises to enforce the Act. They do not have to seek the practice's or anyone else's permission, neither do they have to give notice of their visits. However, they may only enter at a 'reasonable time'.

Inspectors normally give notice of their visits and ring to make an appointment. Occasionally, however, some visits are 'reactive' in response to a complaint from an employee or even a patient. Sometimes inspectors have made unannounced visits, not because they intend to cause offence or 'catch' anybody off guard but simply to slot the inspection of some small premises into a day's schedule of visits to larger premises. Although a surprise visit may be disconcerting, it should not be assumed that the inspector has an ulterior motive. It is because inspections of surgeries are still a fairly rare event that some upset has been caused to those so far affected.

During an investigation the inspector can interview and take written statements from anyone who may have relevant information (and this could include patients as well as staff). The inspector may want to obtain information to establish the facts about an accident or for evidence in legal proceedings. Any information provided will normally be treated as confidential. The information, however, may be subsequently disclosed if a prosecution is brought against the employer.

What do inspectors look for?

Inspectors will wish to ensure that the practice, if employing five or more people, has issued a statement of general policy on health and safety and any relevant instruction on safety procedures. Since 1993, they have also looked for compliance with the requirement to carry out a risk assessment under the Management of Health and Safety at Work Regulations 1992. Increasingly, inspectors are looking for evidence of a good general approach to the management of health and safety. But among specific requirements they will look for some of the following. They will expect an accident book to be kept on the premises. They will want to ensure that all electrical equipment is in safe working order and properly maintained. The normal standards applying to toilet and washing facilities in offices and shops should be met in the practice premises. Inspectors will undoubtedly expect to find a supply of hot and cold running water, and they may also recommend that wrist operated taps should be fitted in rooms used for examination and treatment of patients. They are also concerned about the condition of the heating plant, the arrangements for the storage of drugs, the condition of steam sterilizers, the standards of heating and lighting and the procedure for the disposal of clinical waste. The *Statement of Fees and Allowances* (the Red Book) provides for the direct reimbursement of any charges levied for the disposal of trade waste (see para 51.12(b)).

Improvement and prohibition notices

After completing the inspection the inspector will usually approach the person in administrative charge of the premises (often the practice manager) about any improvements to safety procedures and standards that may be required. If these are minor the inspector will simply ask for them to be put right. If there is something more serious he or she may write formally or may serve a written notice requiring matters to be remedied.

This is known as an improvement notice; it will specify a time limit of not less than 21 days within which the improvement must be made. The inspector must inform staff as well as the employer of the intention to serve this notice. A prosecution alleging a specific breach of a statutory provision may also be brought.

If there is a serious risk to health and safety an inspector may issue a prohibition notice prohibiting the offending work activity. If the position is very grave the notice will take immediate effect and work must stop at once; otherwise, a deferred prohibition notice may be issued stopping the work after a specified time.

The improvement and prohibition notices are both served on the person carrying out or in control of the work in question, and this is normally done at the time of the inspection. The inspector should also advise of the procedure of appeal against the provision of the notice. The notice is normally served on the GPs themselves, unless control of the practice has been delegated to a practice manager. When complied with, notices cease.

Offences and penalties

Because the Health and Safety at Work Act is a criminal statute, contravention of its provisions may lead to a fine or imprisonment. Both the employer and their staff (as well as any other person on the premises) may be liable to prosecution. Furthermore, failure to carry out any duty under the Act is an offence and could also lead to prosecution. Verbal or written warnings, however, such as improvement notices, always precede any legal action. It is also an offence to obstruct inspectors in the performance of their duties and to contravene an improvement or prohibition notice.

The HSE, as the enforcing authority, has the discretion to decide whether or not to prosecute and this decision is taken after advice from the inspector. Alongside a criminal prosecution of an employer, an employee could sue the employer for damages on the basis of employer's liability law or simply for negligence. In any prosecution by the Executive account will be taken of what was reasonably practicable in the circumstances. This offers little consolation to a larger employer but some comfort to the smaller employer with limited resources.

Crown premises – health centres

Although a health authority is a Crown body, it no longer enjoys certain exemptions from prosecution under the Act. Changes in health and safety legislation introduced in 1987 removed Crown immunity from NHS premises.

Fire precautions

Although the Fire Precautions Act 1971 is distinct from the Health and Safety at Work Act, practices should be aware of its requirements. They and their employees, together with any other people working on the premises, must for their own safety and for the safety of others see that there are adequate means of escape (unlocked, unobstructed and usable when people are in the building) and also adequate fire-fighting equipment that is properly maintained and readily available.

In large buildings where more than 20 people work or where more than 10 people work other than on the ground floor, the owner of the premises is required to obtain a certificate from the local fire authority regulating the means of escape and marking of fire exits. If the premises are owned by a health authority they are deemed to be Crown property, and the fire authority would be the Home Office, Scottish Home and Health Department or Welsh Office. These premises should be equipped with properly maintained alarms and the employees should be familiar with the means of escape and the routine to be followed in the event of a fire, and they should have emergency lighting if this is necessary. Local fire inspectors ensure that premises comply with these statutory requirements. If you are in any doubt whether your premises require certification you should contact the fire prevention office of your local fire brigade.

Points to act on

- You should prepare a written safety policy for all employees. Although this is mandatory only for those with five or more employees it is advisable for all practices to prepare such a statement, even if it is brief and simple. This may be included in the employee's employment contract.
- You should carry out a risk assessment for any significant hazards in your workplace. If you have five employees or more, this should be written down.
- Regularly check any obviously hazardous areas – for example, unfinished building work, electrical equipment, loose floor covering – to see if there is anything that needs immediate attention.
- An accident book and copies of the accident report form should be kept in an easily accessible place.
- Ensure that electrical equipment is regularly maintained and serviced.
- Consider appointing a 'safety officer'; the practice manager may be the most appropriate person to do this job.

- Look at your lease or licence agreement to see who is responsible for the upkeep and repair of the premises. Consult your practice solicitor or the BMA if there is any doubt.
- Warning notices should inform patients and visitors of any hazards.

COSHH regulations

The Control of Substances Hazardous to Health (COSHH) set out a legal framework for managing health risks from exposure to hazardous substances used at work. They aim to prevent occupational ill health by encouraging employers to assess and prevent or control risks from exposure to hazardous substances in a systematic and practical way.

These regulations apply to most hazardous substances except those covered by their own legislation, such as asbestos, lead and material producing ionizing radiation. They set out the measures that employers, the self-employed and sometimes employees have to take. Failure to comply exposes employees to risk and constitutes an offence under the Health and Safety at Work Act. Hazardous substances include those labelled as dangerous (i.e. very toxic, toxic, harmful, irritant or corrosive) under other statutory requirements as well as harmful micro-organisms and other biological agents.

What are employers required to do? The basic principles of occupational hygiene underlie the COSHH regulations. These include:

- assessing the risk to health arising from work and what precautions are needed
- introducing measures to prevent or control exposure
- ensuring that control measures are used, equipment is properly maintained and procedures observed
- monitoring where necessary the exposure of employees and carrying out a suitable form of health surveillance where appropriate
- informing, instructing and training employees about the risks and the precautions to be taken.

All employers need to consider how COSHH applies to their employees and working environment. For most practices compliance should be simple and straightforward. More detailed information on COSHH is available from your local HSE office.

Health and safety regulations

Six additional sets of regulations came into force in 1993. They apply to virtually all kinds of work activity, including general practice. Like existing health and safety law, these new regulations require employers to protect both their employees and other persons, including members of the public.

These new regulations have been introduced to both implement EU directives and update existing law. They cover:

* general health and safety management
* work equipment safety
* manual handling of loads
* workplace conditions
* personal protective equipment
* display screen equipment.

Most of the duties laid down by the regulations are not entirely new. They merely clarify and make more explicit what is already health and safety law. Any practice already complying with the Act and its regulations should have no difficulty dealing with the new regulations. But there are some new approaches, especially in relation to the management of health and safety and use of VDUs, which may have to be taken into account.

General health and safety management

These regulations set out broad general duties which, of course, apply to general practices in as much as they are employers. They are aimed at improving health and safety management. If you are already thorough in your approach to your duties under the HSW Act, they should be easy to get to grips with and cause no problems.

The regulations require all employers to:

* assess the risk to the health and safety of employees and to anyone else who may be affected by their work activity. This is so that they can identify any necessary preventive and protective measures. Employers with five or more employees must write down the significant findings of their risk assessment. (This same threshold is already used in the HSW Act: employers with five or more employees have to prepare a written safety policy)

- make arrangements for putting into practice the preventive and protective measures that follow from the risk assessment: they will have to cover planning, organization, control, monitoring and review (i.e. the management of health and safety).

Again, any practice with five or more employees (do not forget that each part-time employee counts as one and also to include your GP registrar or clinical assistant) must record these arrangements:

- carry out health surveillance of employees where the risk assessment shows it to be necessary
- appoint a competent person (normally an employee) to help devise and apply the protective steps shown to be necessary by the risk assessment
- set up emergency procedures
- give employees comprehensible information about health and safety matters
- cooperate on health and safety matters with other employers sharing the premises (e.g. the health authority)
- make sure employees have adequate health and safety training and are capable enough at their job to avoid risk
- provide certain health and safety information to temporary staff to meet their specific needs.

These regulations also:

- place duties on all employees to follow health and safety instructions and report danger; and
- extend current health and safety law which requires you to consult employees' safety representatives and provide facilities for them.

All these general duties exist alongside the more specific ones laid down in other health and safety regulations, including the more recent ones described below. Of course, this does not mean you have to do things twice. For example, if you have done a risk assessment to comply with the Control of Substances Hazardous to Health (COSHH) regulations, you do not need to repeat the exercise to comply with those new general management regulations.

Provision and use of work equipment

These regulations pull together and tidy up a variety of laws governing equipment used at work; instead of piecemeal legislation covering particular kinds of equipment in different industries, these:

- place general duties on all employers; and
- list minimum requirements for work equipment to deal with selected hazards which apply across all industries and sectors.

In general, these regulations make explicit what is already provided for somewhere in current legislation or in good practice. If you have well-chosen and well-maintained equipment you should not need to do any more. Guidance on the regulations reinforces this point. In a few instances some older equipment may need to be upgraded to meet the specific requirements below, but you have had until 1997 to do the necessary work. You should not allow yourself to be bamboozled by any local tradespeople who try to frighten you into employing them to undertake health and safety checks.

Box 14.2: Work equipment

'Work equipment' is broadly defined to include everything from a hand tool, through machines of all kinds, to a complete plant such as an oil refinery. 'Use' includes starting, stopping, installing, dismantling, programming, setting, transporting, maintaining, servicing and cleaning.

These regulations require you to:

- take into account the working conditions and hazards in your surgery when choosing equipment
- in selecting equipment and putting it to use, take into account any risks to health and safety it may pose
- make sure your equipment is suitable for its intended use and that it is properly maintained
- give adequate information, instruction and training.

Specific requirements cover, where appropriate:

- guarding dangerous parts of machinery (replacing the current law on this)
- maintenance arrangements

- dangers caused by equipment failure
- parts and materials at high or very low temperatures
- control systems and devices
- isolation of equipment from power sources
- physical stability of equipment
- lighting
- warnings and markings.

These regulations implement an EU directive aimed at those who select and use work equipment. There are other directives setting out the conditions which much *new* equipment must satisfy before it can be sold in EU member states. These are implemented in the United Kingdom by Government regulations. Any equipment which satisfies these latter regulations is considered to have satisfied the relevant specific requirements listed above.

Manual handling

These regulations replace patchy, old-fashioned and largely ineffective legislation with a modern ergonomic approach to the problem. They are important because the incorrect handling of loads causes many injuries, resulting in pain, time off work and even permanent disablement.

They apply to any manual handling operations which may cause injury at work; these should have been identified by the risk assessment carried out under the general health and safety management regulations described above. They include not only the lifting of loads, but also lowering, pushing, pulling, carrying or moving them, whether by hand or other bodily force. Again these regulations are supported by general guidance.

There are healthcare areas where staff are at risk in this respect – an obvious example is nursing.

You have to take three key steps:

- avoid hazardous manual handling operations where reasonably practicable
- assess adequately any hazardous operations that cannot be avoided
- reduce the risk of injury as far as practicable.

Health, safety and welfare at work

These regulations tidy up a lot of existing legislation, replacing some 35 pieces of old law, including parts of the Factories Act 1961 and the

Offices, Shops and Railway Premises Act 1963. They are much easier to understand, making it far clearer what is expected of you. They cover many aspects of health, safety and welfare in the workplace, setting general requirements in four broad areas.

Working environment

- Temperature.
- Ventilation.
- Lighting including emergency lighting.
- Room dimensions.
- Suitability of workstations.

Safety

- Safe passage of pedestrians and vehicles (e.g. traffic routes must be wide enough and properly marked).
- Windows and skylights (safe opening, closing and cleaning).
- Transparent/translucent doors and partitions (use of safe material and marking).
- Doors, gates and escalators (safety devices).
- Floors (construction and maintenance, obstructions and slipping and tripping hazards).
- Falls from height.
- Falling objects (e.g. from cupboards or shelves).

Facilities

- Toilets.
- Washing, eating and changing facilities.
- Clothing storage.
- Seating.
- Rest areas (and arrangements in them for non-smokers).
- Rest facilities for pregnant women and nursing mothers.

Housekeeping

- Maintenance of workplace, equipment and facilities.
- Cleanliness.
- Removal of waste materials.

You have to ensure that your surgery complies with the regulations; this should have been completed by 1996. Other people connected with your surgery premises (e.g. the owner of a building which is leased to one or more employers or self-employed people) also have to ensure that requirements falling within their control are satisfied. Again these regulations are supported by an approved code of practice.

Personal protective equipment

These regulations set out sound principles for selecting, providing, maintaining and using personal protective equipment.

Personal protective equipment (known as PPE) should be relied on only as a last resort. But where risks are adequately controlled by other means you have a duty to provide suitable equipment, free of charge, for all employees exposed to those risks. Personal protective equipment is suitable only if it is appropriate for the risks and the working conditions, takes account of staff needs and fits them properly, gives adequate protection and is compatible with any other PPE they may wear.

Box 14.3: Personal protective equipment

'Personal protective equipment' is defined as all equipment designed to be worn or held to protect against a risk to health or safety. It includes most types of protective clothing and equipment such as eye, foot and head protection, safety harness, life jackets and high visibility clothing. There are some exceptions, e.g. ordinary working clothes and uniforms (including clothes provided for food hygiene), those provided for road transport (for example, crash helmets) and sports equipment.

You also have duties to:

- assess the risks and PPE you intend to issue to ensure that it is suitable
- maintain, clean and replace PPE
- provide storage for PPE when not being used
- ensure PPE is properly used
- give training, information and instruction on its use.

All new PPE must comply with an EU directive on design, certification and testing. This is implemented in the United Kingdom by regulations made by the Department of Trade and Industry, but you are allowed to use PPE bought before the implementation of these regulations.

VDU health and safety regulations

Unlike most of the other regulations outlined in this chapter, the Health and Safety (Display Screen Equipment) Regulations do not replace old legislation but cover a new area of work activity for the first time. Generally, working with VDUs is not a high risk activity, but it can lead to musculoskeletal problems, eye fatigue and mental stress. Problems of this kind can be overcome by good ergonomic design of equipment, furniture, the working environment and the tasks performed.

The regulations apply to those VDUs where there is a 'user', i.e. an employee who habitually uses it as a significant part of normal work, and to employers who have some duties towards self-employed 'operators' using their workstations. They cover equipment used for the display of text, numbers and graphics regardless of the display process used.

Your duties include:

- assessing VDU workstations and reducing risks that are identified
- making sure workstations satisfy minimum requirements set for the VDU itself, keyboard, desk and chair, working environment and task design and software
- planning VDU work so that there are breaks or changes in activity
- providing information and training for VDU users.

Employers must also provide VDU users on request with appropriate eye and eyesight tests, and special glasses if they are needed and normal ones cannot be used. Again, these regulations are supported by detailed guidelines.

Appendix A: GMSC guidelines on avoiding violence against GPs and practice staff

Introduction

GPs and their staff have come to accept a measure of verbal abuse and physical violence as intrinsic to the job. This unacceptable behaviour should not have to be tolerated. The problem is not confined to deprived areas and occurs in both rural and urban areas.

If we fail to take vigorous action in the face of actual or threatened violence, we will not only be doing a disservice to ourselves, our staff and other colleagues, but we will be allowing the essential foundation of mutual trust upon which our primary care system is based to be put at risk.

If abusive or violent behaviour towards a doctor is tolerated, the perpetrator has no incentive to refrain from such behaviour. Furthermore, his or her children and peers are likely to emulate the behaviour and thereby perpetuate the problem.

A firm policy aimed at preventing violent and threatening behaviour must now become an integral part of our professionalism.

The GMSC has prepared this guidance and hopes that practices will act upon it without delay. We are approaching the Department to seek amendments to the regulations to further strengthen the position of the GP when dealing with abuse and violence.

Prevention

Advice to GPs from the Association of Chief Police Officers is at Annex 1 (Appendix B). The following advice supplements this.

1 Ensure your own behaviour is beyond reproach and does not contribute to the development of an abusive or violent incident. Specific staff training, an adequate and flexible appointment system and a prompt explanation of any delay can help to avoid threatening and violent behaviour.
2 Inevitably there will be occasions when the seemingly unreasonable demands of a patient, coupled with your own fatigue, may lead you to be very annoyed. If you feel yourself getting angry, try to calm down before seeing the patient. Try to avoid remonstrating with the patient at the time. Every practice should have a written policy (agreed by all partners) on what procedures should be followed, e.g. writing to any patient who makes unnecessary calls, summary removal from the list of anyone abusing the GPs or their staff, and calling the police to deal with anyone who is physically violent.

It is important to realize that some patients who behave reasonably towards their own personal doctor are abusive to others in the practice. All GPs should be prepared to take action even if they are not themselves the recipient of abusive or violent behaviour.

3 Your appearance when making house calls can be important. In some areas, new or conspicuous cars or outward signs of your professional status can attract unwelcome attention. Some of our colleagues prefer to use a comparatively unobtrusive vehicle and wear more casual clothes, carrying any medical equipment in a pocket rather than in the conventional bag.

4 Try to ensure good relations are maintained with your local police force, both at practice level and through the LMC. They should be able to cooperate in your practice plan for preventing violence, which may include:
  • arranging for police to accompany partners to home visits where there is any threat of violence
  • if all else fails and urgent medical care seems essential and requires a home visit, call both an ambulance and the police, and refer the patient to accident and emergency, warning all parties of your fears. It would be difficult to find a doctor in breach of the terms of service for doing this, since referral is a proper course of action for a GP.

5 If street lighting is poor or the numbering and naming of roads and residences is inadequate, press your local authority to act.

6 You may wish to consider taking advice from a reputable security firm; they may suggest fitting a continuous recording video unit in reception and alarm systems in consulting rooms.

7 You may wish to include in your practice leaflet a carefully drafted paragraph (perhaps supplemented by a notice in your reception area) outlining your policy for dealing with threats or incidents of violence. This can be presented as expressing your practice's responsibility to all patients, since most of them would be disturbed by an abusive or violent incident.

8 In the case of 'no-go' areas where the police are unable to offer effective protection, the LMC, health authority and police should agree jointly on how medical care can be provided on a basis which ensures the safety of GPs.

9 If you show you are determined to initiate a criminal prosecution, this can be an effective deterrent to others, particularly those who wish to avoid any further involvement with the police.

What action to take following a threatening or violent incident

You should always make an official complaint to the police following a violent or threatening episode. This policy already applies in virtually all hospital accident and emergency departments. The issue of confidentiality does not prevent you from divulging the circumstances of the incident (the medical aspects of the consultation must, of course, remain confidential).

Under current criminal law,* the alleged offence will be subject to different legislation according to whether it occurs in a 'dwelling house' (e.g. the patient's home) or in a 'public place' (e.g. the surgery).

Incidents in the surgery

Provided that the incident does not occur in a dwelling house, Section 4 of the Public Order Act 1986 makes it an offence '...to use towards another person threatening, abusive or insulting words or behaviour with intent to cause that person to believe that immediate unlawful violence will be used against him or by any person'.

Section 5 of the same Act makes it an offence '...to use threatening, abusive or insulting words or behaviour within the hearing or sight of a person likely to be caused harassment, alarm or distress'.

Incidents in the patient's home

The Public Order Act 1986 referred to above unfortunately does not apply to incidents which occur in a 'dwelling house', consequently GPs do not have the same protection against such behaviour if it occurs in a patient's home.

In the event of an actual assault, however, the Offences Against the Person Act applies; under this statute there are offences of assault and assault occasioning actual bodily harm (touching someone without their consent can constitute assault). These offences apply to both the home and the surgery. You should not hesitate in invoking the law, particularly since these kinds of offence involve a more serious level of threatening or violent behaviour than the public order offences.

How to prosecute

Hopefully the police will prosecute in cases involving the types of offences described above. If they do not you may consider bringing a private prosecution in a magistrates court.

* All references to legislation relate to the position in England and Wales.

To issue a summons against an individual you must apply to the local magistrates court. Although it can normally be issued at the start of each day's business, it is advisable to contact the magistrates court first. After the summons has been issued the GP has to arrange for it to be served on the individual concerned; this is normally done by using an inquiry agent if you do not want to do so personally.

Terminating professional responsibility

A GP will almost always consider that the doctor–patient relationship, which is based on mutual trust, has been terminated by abusive, threatening or violent behaviour, and will want to remove the patient from the list as soon as possible. This can be done by writing to the health authority asking for the patient's removal after an interval of seven days. (This procedure applies to all categories of NHS patients, including temporary patients.)

In some rural areas where patients can use only one practice, GPs sometimes feel this action is pointless. However, experience has shown that the very act of removal and reallocation back to the same list can serve to foster a more positive patient–doctor relationship.

In the circumstances of an assault it is possible to obtain an injunction ex parte to stop a defendant from further molesting, assaulting or contacting the GP or practice. Your application to a county court judge should be supported by an affidavit setting out the grounds for requesting the injunction. If violence or injury is involved the injunction may well have a penal endorsement, e.g. if the defendant breaches the order he or she may be arrested and brought before the court for contempt. The injunction is, in theory, a first step in proceedings against a defendant to obtain damages for an assault or threat of violence. It may be obtained urgently and at short notice and before proceedings have been issued; however, an undertaking will need to be given that proceedings will be issued without delay. A solicitor will almost certainly be necessary. (LMCs may wish to advise on local solicitors with expertise in this field.) Once granted, the injunction must be served personally on the defendant and there will then be a further court hearing (usually seven days later). A copy of the injunction should be sent to the police. Such injunctions are commonly used for incidents of domestic violence and overcome police reluctance to intervene. Any breach of an injunction can lead to a fine or imprisonment for contempt of court.

Because there is a seven-day limit before the patient can be removed at a doctor's request, there will be occasions when doctors need to stop any further contact with the patient. In these circumstances the injunction should restrain the patient from communicating in any way with the practice. This course of action is not as illogical as it sounds; whereas a removal from the list at the doctor's request takes a week, the patient may choose to find another doctor at any time. Using an injunction to stop the patient from seeing one practice does not prevent medical care being obtained elsewhere by finding another doctor.

Before the patient is removed, house calls should be avoided. If you use the procedure suggested above, any disorder that may occur will be in a 'public place' and therefore not be subject to the 'dwelling house' exclusion of the Public Order Act.

Since all the above offences are arrestable, essential medical care for violent persons subsequent to their arrest is available from police surgeons or the prison medical service.

Any doctor who removes a patient from the list following violence or abuse should tell the LMC secretary, who should warn other doctors in the locality to exercise great care if they treat the patient.

The GMSC believes the seven-day rule is no longer tolerable in cases of assault or serious abuse involving threats, and we are seeking to persuade Government to agree to change the relevant regulation. In the meantime, although we cannot advise GPs to breach their terms of service, we realize that some will feel unable to comply with them following a request for immediate removal. This eventuality is highly undesirable and underlines the need to change the GP's terms of service in this respect.

Offences relating to drug procurement

Some attacks on GPs are drug related, often resulting from their refusal to agree to prescribe (often for a temporary resident) a particular drug. Firm action to prosecute anyone using threatening behaviour or deception for these purposes soon becomes known within the drug subculture, and can help to give a practice the reputation of being an unattractive destination for anyone not genuinely seeking help for a drug-related condition.

A false temporary or permanent address, a falsely named GP and false clinical information can be checked by contacting the named GP. Successful prosecutions leading to imprisonment have been achieved for trying to obtain prescription-only medicines or controlled drugs by deceit.

The use of threatening or violent behaviour to obtain drugs is even more serious. If a prescription is issued under such threat, the police and local pharmacies should be told immediately; they may use a network of contacts to pass the information on and also delay dispensing until the police arrive.

Conclusion

The advice in this document may seem to be contrary to our duty to provide care and uphold patient confidentiality. Sadly, the need for it has been caused by social and cultural changes beyond our influence or control. Indeed, if we fail to use the law to uphold the doctor–patient relationship, we may find that its value inexorably declines.

If we are all resolute in our determination to counteract abuse and violence, the message will soon spread that GPs will not tolerate this type of behaviour.

Appendix B: Avoiding assaults: Association of Chief Police Officers' advice to general practitioners and community health officials

Surgery

1 Take appropriate advice from your local crime prevention officer on the protection of your premises against intruders and thefts by patients.
2 Train your staff to be aware of crime risks and to identify and deal with persons who have become aggressive or show signs of doing so.
3 Examine your appointment procedures to see if anything may be done to alleviate frustrations and boredom which may lead to violence.
4 Advise your staff on interpersonal skills.
5 The layout and design of the surgery is important in putting patients at ease and eliminating boredom. A clearly identifiable reception and attractive surroundings are helpful. 'Blind corners', poor lighting and furnishings which could be used as weapons should be avoided. Further guidance on these points has been drawn up by the ACPO and is available on request.
6 Have secure storage for your drugs and prescription forms and a secure procedure for their use:
   • don't pre-sign
   • don't pre-stamp
   • don't leave in open waiting room for collection
   • specimen signature to local chemists
   • don't leave prescription pads unattended in your consulting rooms.

In the community

1 Recognize a risk of crime and be observant when in known crime areas. If unsure, try and minimize the risk and ask for a police escort.
2 Carry drugs in your pockets, wherever possible, or in a security bag with alarm.
3 Don't display 'Doctor on Call'/'Nurse on Call' sticker in your vehicle at night and only during the day if necessary to avoid wheel clamping.
4 Keep personal valuables in your possession to a minimum.
5 Consider the use of personal radio or radio telephone to call assistance if attacked.
6 Tell your office where you are going to be and arrange a system of contact at set intervals in areas of known risk.
7 Ascertain from the patient requesting your attention if there are certain difficulties in that area; perhaps one of the family can meet you and protect your vehicle whilst you are engaged with the call.
8 Make sure new staff are aware of risk areas and families.
9 Note risk patients in patient register.
10 Liaise with local police on current risks.
11 Consider the use of members of voluntary schemes (neighbourhood watch) as escorts.

In your car

1 When driving at night keep to well lit main roads as far as possible and lock all the doors.
2 Don't give lifts and if in fear of being followed go to the nearest police station.
3 Park your car in a well lit area and have a good look around before getting out. Have your car ready on your return and check the interior of the car before getting in.
4 Don't leave anything of value or drugs on open view – take them with you or secure them in a container of appropriate design which is securely bolted to the floor of the vehicle. (Note, you are at risk whilst reaching down into the boot so fit the storage receptacle inside the car.)

15 Statutory sick pay

Basic principles • Outline of SSP scheme • How it works • Who is eligible to receive SSP? • Deciding when to pay • How should it be paid? • Claiming back SSP • When to stop paying SSP • Points to act on • Keeping records

Where to obtain advice and assistance

Your first point of contact should be the Social Security advice line on 0800 393539; for more information contact your local Social Security office. If in dispute about any matter concerning SSP, BMA members should contact their local BMA office.

The Social Security and Housing Benefits Act 1982 imposes a statutory duty on employers to pay staff during sickness absences on behalf of the state. Prior to the introduction of the statutory sick pay (SSP) scheme, sick pay as such had not been covered by legislation. Employers had discretion to decide whether or not to pay staff during sickness absences; the only constraint on how this discretion was exercised had been any obligations arising from their contracts of employment.

When writing about any legislation it is particularly rewarding to suggest a course of action that can be easily understood and readily applied in general practice. A first impression of SSP may be that it is complicated and difficult to administer. But if its basic principles are understood and a few simple preliminary and precautionary steps taken, practices are unlikely to have serious difficulties. Advice and assistance may be obtained from your BMA local office or your local Social Security office.

In common with other employment law SSP pays little regard to the limited resources of small employers. General practice has a far greater relative burden of additional administration and this often has to be borne by the practice manager. The DSS booklet *Statutory Sick Pay: Manual for*

Employers is essential reading and may be obtained from your local DSS office. This authoritative guide to the scheme is an essential document when you have to pay sickness benefit. You should also obtain a supply of DSS forms for 'transfer', 'exclusion' and 'leaving' and your sickness records should conform to the statutory requirements. Do not try to memorize the details of the scheme. It is through the practical experience of working out actual cases of the sickness scheme that you become familiar with it. Administering the scheme should be a routine procedure, almost as familiar as PAYE.

It is reasonable to assume that many practices do not have a formal sick pay scheme. Instead, they probably take a pragmatic approach when determining what pay staff should receive during absence for sickness. They may even maintain staff on full pay for short periods of absence, though this may mean that such staff, if they should claim state sickness benefit, could have been financially better off during sickness than when working.

But when the period of sickness lengthens a practice's decision to reduce or end sick pay may depend on various subjective considerations, including the value attached to the previous service of the sick employee, the length of previous service and the likelihood of the employee's returning to work within the foreseeable future. Many practices may not have planned ahead for long-term sickness because they regard it as a remote eventuality.

Basic principles

The SSP scheme establishes a minimum entitlement for sick pay for most employees. It replaced state sickness benefit for most periods of short-term sickness absence. The employer is required to pay sickness benefit as the agent of the Government, but the decision on whether sick pay should be paid lies primarily with the employer rather than the DSS. This statutory entitlement, however, does not prevent additional payments being made under an occupational sick pay scheme alongside SSP (or for those periods of sickness absence not covered by SSP). Indeed, a single payment may be made by the employer to cover both SSP and any occupational sick pay entitlements. The Act allows employers to offset their liability to pay SSP against any contractual liability for sick pay.

How does 'offsetting' work? If you are committed by contract to pay your employee for a day on which the employee was sick – for example, your practice's scheme for occupational sick pay or holiday pay – this payment will cover your liability for SSP so long as the amount you are paying is at least the appropriate level for that scheme. You do not have to pay SSP as well. More generally, if SSP is due to be paid on a certain day any other payment that counts as earnings for the purposes of National Insurance (NI) contributions that you are already liable to make on that day will count towards your liability to pay SSP for that day.

The Social Security and Housing Benefits Act represented a radical new approach to sickness benefits in that:

- all staff are covered by the Act and are entitled to SSP instead of state sickness or injury benefit for most periods of sickness unless for some reason they are excluded, and all employers are legally obliged to pay SSP
- for those staff not covered by your own sick pay arrangements the statutory scheme is usually their only source of income during sickness unless they qualify in addition for supplementary benefits
- staff covered by your own occupational sick pay arrangements may continue to receive a higher level of sick pay than that due under the statutory scheme
- both the statutory scheme and your own sick pay is paid by the practice
- long-term sickness is still covered by the present NI scheme, and staff will normally transfer from SSP to state invalidity benefit after 28 weeks' entitlement to SSP has been used up.

Outline of SSP scheme

The main features of the scheme are:

- NI sickness benefit is not payable for most sickness absence; instead your staff should receive SSP directly from you
- SSP is paid in the same way as normal pay and is liable to deductions for income tax and NI contributions
- entitlement to SSP does not depend on previous NI contributions or previous service with the employer
- married women paying the reduced 'stamp' and part-timers are entitled to sick pay provided that their earnings are above £64 a week. SSP is not paid for sickness during the first three unlinked waiting days, but for longer absences it will be paid for up to 28 weeks' worth. After 28 weeks of SSP state benefit may be claimed from the DSS

- if an employee changes jobs the new employer may also be liable to pay up to 28 weeks' SSP, but should check whether payments have been made by the previous employer
- you, as the employer, have to decide whether SSP is payable
- the amount of SSP any employer can recover is governed by the percentage threshold scheme (*see* below).

How it works

Employers are responsible for paying SSP to their employees for the first 28 weeks of sickness or injury. There is now a single flat rate (£57.70 per week) which applies to all employees irrespective of whether they are paying class 1 NI contributions or the lower 'stamp' under the current NI benefit scheme. But there is no requirement to pay SSP if average earnings are below the NI lower earnings limit, which is currently £64 a week. (To calculate average earnings, the general rule is to add together earnings over the 12 weeks up to and including the last pay before the period of incapacity for work began and then to divide the total by 12. Any payment that is treated as earnings for the purpose of NI contributions must be included and the gross figure – before NI or other deductions are made – must be used.)

At the end of 28 weeks of SSP, the DSS normally accepts responsibility for payment of sickness or injury benefit (except for employees who pay the married women's reduced NI rate) which is dependant related and tax free.

The rules for determining when payments for sickness absence should be made are set out in the DSS's *Statutory Sick Pay: Manual for Employers*. The checklist below will help a practice to decide when payments should be made. An employee's entitlement to SSP depends on three main conditions.

1 That the day of absence forms part of a *period of incapacity for work* – any four or more consecutive calendar days when the employee is incapable of doing work of a type that they might reasonably be expected to do under the contract of employment due to specific disease or bodily or mental disablement constitute a period of incapacity for work.
2 That the day of absence is part of a *period of entitlement* – that is, during which the employee would be expected to carry out the continuing contract of employment, not having exhausted entitlement to sick pay or

being excluded for certain other reasons from entitlement to it; a period of entitlement will occur in most cases.

3 That the day is a *qualifying day* – that is, a day or days on which the employee would normally be contractually required by the practice to be available for work or which is agreed between the practice and the employee to reflect the terms of that contract. In most circumstances qualifying days will be those days normally worked.

Statutory sick pay, together with any payments made under occupational sick pay schemes (except for those schemes based on trusts and insurance companies), is subject to PAYE (income tax) and to employer's and employee's NI contributions, just like normal pay. It is also permissible to make other deductions from SSP, such as the employee's contributions to an occupational pension scheme, savings arrangements or any other deductions that are made under normal circumstances from an employee's pay.

Who is eligible to receive SSP?

In general all employees are covered by SSP if they are sick for four or more consecutive days. But there are circumstances when there is no liability to pay (*see* Box 15.1). When employees in one of these groups are off sick they must be told why they are not being paid for sickness absence so that they can claim state sickness benefit instead. The law requires you to complete an 'exclusion form' and give or send it to the employee (together with any sick notes) not later than seven days after you have been notified of sickness. This form tells the employee and the DSS why you are not paying for sickness absence and provides the employee with a claim form for state sickness benefit. You are of course free to pay your own sick pay to any employee not eligible to receive SSP.

Deciding when to pay

You may first know of the employee's sick absence when they do not come to work. You will expect the employee to report the absence (*see* Box 15.2) and if, according to the SSP regulations, notification is late you may opt to withhold sick pay (*see* Box 15.3). But you should be very cautious about withholding SSP; no action should be taken before seeking advice from

---

Box 15.1: Who does not receive SSP?

You do not have to pay an employee who:

- is over minimum state pension age at the time of going sick *or*
- was taken on for a short-term contract of three months or less *or*
- has average weekly earnings less than the lower limit for NI contribution liability *or*
- goes sick within 57 days of a previous claim for one of these state benefits: sickness benefit, invalidity pension, maternity allowance and unemployment benefit *or*
- has done no work for you under the contract of service *or*
- is within the 'disqualifying' period related to her pregnancy *or*
- has already had 28 weeks' SSP with a previous employer *or*
- is outside the European Community *or*
- is in legal custody *or*
- goes sick during a stoppage of work, unless he or she has not taken part in the dispute and has no direct interests in it

---

your DSS office. If SSP is withheld you must formally notify your employee, who may then appeal against your decision through the DSS office.

You may not need to change your present rules for reporting sickness absence. But if these are more stringent than the SSP regulations require, an employee regarded as late in notifying sickness for your purposes may not be late for SSP purposes. You are entitled to ask for reasonable evidence of incapacity. The type of evidence required for SSP and when it may be requested are summarized in Box 15.4.

For the purposes of determining when SSP is payable, a day of sickness is a day on which the employee is incapable, because of a specific illness or disablement, of doing work that they can reasonably be expected to do under their contract of employment. Only complete days of sickness count for the scheme.

Before SSP is owing there must be four or more consecutive days of sickness. Sundays and public holidays are included in this calculation. (Thus, if an employee has a short spell of sickness just before or after a weekend you will need to know whether they were incapable of work on Saturday and Sunday.) This is called a 'period of incapacity for work'. If there are

Box 15.2: Notifying sickness absence

Employers usually have rules about the time by which an employee should notify sickness. Your current arrangements may be appropriate for the purpose of the SSP scheme; its regulations provide that:

- you must make it clear to your employees how you want to be notified of sickness, e.g. by telephone, in writing or both
- you may not require notification earlier than the first qualifying day in a period of sickness
- you may not require notification by a specific time on the first qualifying day
- notification in writing must be regarded as having been made on the day of posting
- notification may be made by proxy
- you may not *require* notification in the form of medical evidence
- you may not require notification more often than once a week during sickness.

You do not need to change your practice rules but if these are more strict you may find that a notification that is regarded as 'late' by your rules is nevertheless acceptable for the statutory sick pay scheme.

Box 15.3: Late notification of absence

- If an employee is late in notifying sickness without reasonable cause you may withhold sick pay
- But you may only withhold sick pay if there was no good cause for the delay in notification
- Each employer has to apply common sense and judgement in deciding if there was good cause for late notification

---

Box 15.4: Evidence of sickness

- You are entitled to ask for reasonable evidence of incapacity, e.g. a self-certificate for periods of four to seven days or a doctor's statement for periods after the first seven days
- You may use your own self-certification forms
- Your responsibility is to satisfy yourself that your employee is incapable of working under his or her contract; whether you accept the evidence presented is for you to decide
- A certificate of incapacity for work may be received from someone who is not a registered medical practitioner, including osteopaths, chiropractors, Christian Scientists, herbalists and acupuncturists, but 'doctor's statement is strong evidence of incapacity and should usually be accepted as conclusive unless there is evidence to the contrary; e.g. if your employee was said to be incapable of work because of an ankle injury, but was seen playing football'[1]

---

fewer than four consecutive days of sickness there is no 'period of incapacity for work' and no action should be taken under the scheme.

SSP is not necessarily paid for all days in a period of incapacity for work since it has to be paid only for 'qualifying days' of sickness (*see* Box 15.5). Moreover, it is not payable for the first three qualifying days in any period of incapacity since these are the waiting days. For example, your receptionist, who has five agreed qualifying days a week – Monday to Friday inclusive – is sick for one week starting on Monday. If this employee is eligible for sick pay Monday, Tuesday and Wednesday will be waiting days and SSP will be due on Thursday and Friday.

Periods of incapacity for work that are separated by eight weeks – i.e. 56 calendar days – or less are said to be linked: they count together as a single period. Thus, if two or more periods are linked then there can be no more than three waiting days in all.

Your maximum liability to pay SSP is defined as follows. The maximum amount payable is 28 weeks, and liability continues as long as the period of incapacity for work (or linked periods of incapacity) lasts subject to the 28 weeks limit. Separate periods of incapacity are linked as long as they are not separated by more than eight weeks. There is a three year limit to any linking of periods of incapacity. If your employee's sickness continues after your liability for SSP ends they may be able to claim state

---

Box 15.5: Qualifying days

- Qualifying days are the only days for which sick pay is payable, and are the only days that count as waiting days. They are days agreed between you and your employee – these will normally be the days of the week on which an employee is required by his or her contract to be available for work or days chosen to reflect the pattern of working. For example, if your receptionist works on a rota system you may agree qualifying days that follow the pattern of working exactly or you may agree that the same days of each week will be qualifying days

- You are free to choose which days you wish, as long as you and your employee are in agreement. But there is an overriding rule: any agreement must provide at least one qualifying day in each week

- If you cannot reach agreement the qualifying days will be those days on which the employee would actually have worked if he or she had not been sick – but the overriding rule still holds. If your employee would not have worked in a particular week the regulations provide that Wednesday of that week will be regarded as a qualifying day

- In the absence of a clear indication of which days would have been working days in any week the regulations provide that every day of that week, except standard rest days, will be qualifying days

- These rules allow for great flexibility in the way that qualifying days may be agreed with your employees. If you are already committed to paying your own occupational sick pay you should aim at maximizing receipt of sick pay to offset this

---

sickness benefit. To make this transfer to the state scheme as smooth as possible you must give a sick employee a DSS 'transfer form' SSP1.

How should it be paid?

Because SSP can be paid only for qualifying days, the daily rate is the weekly rate divided by the number of qualifying days in the week (beginning with

Sunday). For example, for an employee who works five days a week the agreed qualifying days are Monday to Friday inclusive. Sick pay is normally paid when you would have paid your employee wages for the same period. In most cases you will pay it on the same day that you pay occupational sick pay. The legislation provides for SSP to be offset against any payment that you make from your own occupational sick pay scheme.

Claiming back SSP

The SSP small employers' relief scheme was abolished in 1995 and was replaced by the percentage threshold scheme. The new scheme is designed to help employers who have a high proportion of their workforce sick at any one time, and is not restricted to small businesses. Unless you qualify under the new scheme, you are not entitled to recover any SSP you pay to your employees.

How to work out if you qualify

The percentage threshold scheme applies to all SSP payments for days of incapacity since 6 April 1995. Under the scheme, you must compare the total SSP paid in a tax month with 13% of your total, employers' and employees', gross class 1 NI contributions for that tax month. **Do not include class 1A contributions.** You can get back any SSP paid over and above 13% of your NI liability. Tax months begin on the 6th of each month.

Your class 1 NI liability for a tax month is based on the payments made in that month. To work out if you qualify under the scheme in a tax month in which you paid SSP:

1 work out the total gross class 1 NI contribution liability for the tax month
2 multiply by 13% and round up fractions of a penny
3 work out the total SSP payments in that month.

If the amount at point three is more than the amount at point two, you can recover the difference between the two amounts.

If you qualify in one month, you do not automatically qualify in the next. If an employee's period of incapacity for work (PIW) spans two or more tax months, you must do separate calculations for each month.

Small employers can pay their tax and NI contributions quarterly and will, therefore, recover SSP quarterly. However, they must calculate the amount they are entitled to recover monthly.

When to stop paying SSP

You should not pay SSP to employees for any period after:

- they are no longer incapable of work, e.g. if they return to work or stop sending doctor's statements
- they have been due 28 weeks' SSP at the appropriate weekly rate
- in the case of female staff, the 11th week before the week in which the baby is due
- their contracts of service come to an end
- they go abroad outside the European Union or are taken into legal custody.

Points to act on

There are several steps you should have taken to ensure that your practice complies with the SSP scheme:

- agreed with your staff which days serve as qualifying days. These are usually those days normally worked, including Saturdays if applicable
- decided on a system of notification of illness and told your staff what this is. Your staff must know when you require notification and what evidence of incapacity is required
- obtained a supply of the relevant DSS forms to transfer staff to the NI state benefit scheme, to exclude staff from payment of sick pay and for leavers
- made sure your record keeping complies with what is required under the scheme
- obtained your free copy of the DSS's revised *Statutory Sick Pay: Manual for Employers* which provides an authoritative statement of the scheme[1]
- if you have further doubts or worries the staff of the BMA local offices are available to advise and help BMA members
- if you are already committed to paying your own occupational sick pay you should arrange with your staff the qualifying days so that you may obtain the maximum reimbursement of SSP as a combination towards offsetting your own sick pay.

Keeping records

You are required by law to keep the following sickness absence records:

- dates of sickness absence of at least four consecutive days (including Saturdays and Sundays) reported to you by your employees
- any days within these sickness absences for which SSP was *not* paid, together with the reasons for not paying
- details of each employee's qualifying days in each period of incapacity.

All these records should be kept in a form that allows a DSS inspector access to them on request, and you must be able to produce them within a reasonable time if asked to do so. They are, of course, your own source of information if an employee asks for a written statement of entitlement to SSP for a past period.

As long as the records conform to these requirements they may be kept in any way that is convenient to you. You must retain them for at least three years after the end of the tax year to which they relate. There is a penalty for failure to comply. The DSS has produced a record sheet for the scheme.

You are also required by law to keep records showing, for each pay day and for each employee, any SSP that is paid as well as the usual records of pay, PAYE (income tax) and NI contributions.

In addition to the above records that you are legally obliged to keep there are other records that you may want for your own purposes:

- any doctor's statements or sick notes. You may wish to retain or copy the originals, since if there should be some dispute about days of sickness, knowledge of the date on which the doctor signed the sick note, when you received it, the period it covered and the nature of the illness could be useful
- details of your rules on the notification of sickness and the dates on which your employees notified you of sickness. This information will be useful if there is any dispute about eligibility for SSP.

Unless some adjustment is made to the directly reimbursed salaries of GP registrars and staff who continue to be paid when sick there will be an element of double payment. It has been agreed that:

- trainers should inform health authorities of the amount of SSP paid and recovered so that they can reimburse GP registrars' salaries net of sick pay
- doctors should, when informing health authorities of the salaries paid to staff under the practice staff scheme, specify the amount of SSP paid

and recovered when staff are sick and this will be set against the amount directly reimbursed.

Reference

1 Contributions Agency (1997) **Statutory Sick Pay: Manual for Employers**. Available from local Contributions Agency offices.

16 Redundancy

Where to obtain advice and assistance

Redundancy is often a very difficult matter for employers to handle correctly. BMA members should not hesitate to contact their local BMA office. Local ACAS offices are also able to offer advice.

Genuine redundancy is still rare among practice staff. But unfair dismissals on the pretext of redundancy are, regrettably, more common; it is sometimes thought that redundancy offers a more palatable way of getting rid of an unwanted employee. Changes in general practice, however, have led to genuine redundancies as practices face a decline in income and others change staffing arrangements to meet new demands on their services.

When a redundancy occurs important legal obligations fall upon the employer. Employees have a statutory right to receive redundancy payments and paid time off from work to look for another job if they have at least two years' service. The same qualifying condition also determines whether employees have the right to claim that they have been unfairly dismissed if a redundancy selection has not been made fairly according to objective criteria.

When is a dismissal a redundancy?

Redundancy is defined as a dismissal caused by an employer's need to reduce the number of staff. It may be caused by a closure of a practice or simply a need for fewer staff. Normally an identifiable area of work should have disappeared. A dismissal cannot be regarded as a redundancy if the employer immediately engages a direct replacement; but they may engage an employee with different skills or in a different location (unless the redundant employee could be required under his or her contract of employment to work at that other location). If a health authority partially or wholly withdraws funding from a specific post this could provide legitimate grounds for declaring a redundancy in that post.

In general, to be eligible to receive a redundancy payment the employee should have been dismissed by the employer and will not have resigned on their own initiative. An employee may, however, receive a compensatory payment if the employer has not actually dismissed them but has acted in such a manner that the employee is entitled to leave the job without giving due notice.

If an employer announces that a redundancy will be necessary and invites someone to volunteer as a means of selecting who should go, the employee who volunteers to be dismissed still qualifies for a redundancy payment provided the employer actually dismisses them.

Transfer of one practice to another practice

Normally any employee of a practice, when it changes hands, automatically becomes an employee of the 'successor' practice on the same terms and conditions. It is as if the employee's contract had originally been made with the new practice; continuity of employment is preserved, as are any rights that may have been acquired under the original contract. So when staff are transferred in this way no dismissal has occurred and there is thus no entitlement to a redundancy payment. Because the merger of practices is not uncommon it is important to be aware of this transfer of employment rights, including any right to redundancy payments.

Qualifying for statutory redundancy payments

An employer must make a lump sum payment to any employee with at least two years' continuous service who is dismissed because of redundancy.

Self-employed people or members of a partnership do not qualify, neither does an employee over the age of 65 or an employee who works for an organization with a normal retiring age (for both men and women) of less than 65 and has reached that age. The lump sum diminishes by 1/12 for each month after the age of 64. Employees on fixed term contracts of at least two years' duration which include, with explicit written agreement, a clause waiving entitlement to redundancy payments are also disqualified.

At the time of writing an industrial tribunal has held that rules which deny over-65s the right to claim unfair dismissal or redundancy breach European sex equality law. The tribunal decided that the rules were discriminatory because more men than women want to work after 65. Although tribunal rulings do not set a precedent, if the case is subsequently upheld on appeal it will open up the way for both men and women over age 65 to claim unemployment protection rights.

To qualify for a statutory payment an employee who is dismissed as redundant must have worked for at least two years, but service before the age of 18 years does not count.

A redundant employee may not be entitled to a redundancy payment if a new job is offered within the practice, provided it is offered before the old employment contract ends and begins within four weeks. In this situation an employee can defer a decision on whether to accept the new job for a four week trial period and if they remain in the job at the end of this period it will be assumed that the offer has been accepted. If the four week trial period does not work out then the employee may be made redundant and receive any redundancy payment due. A longer period may apply if retraining is required.

Calculating redundancy payments

The amount of an employee's lump sum statutory redundancy payment depends on how long they have been continuously employed in the practice, how these years of service relate to particular age bands, and on weekly pay. It is calculated by multiplying a week's pay (or half or one and a half times a week's pay, depending on age in each year of service) by the number of complete years of service (*see* Box 16.1). The maximum length of service which may count for this purpose is 20 years, and the maximum week's pay is currently £220: thus the maximum statutory redundancy payment is £6600.

An employee does not pay income tax on a statutory redundancy payment but the employer may set it off against tax as a business expense.

Box 16.1: Calculating redundancy payments

1½ week's pay	For each complete year of employment in which the employee was not below age 41 but was below either age 65 or the organization's normal retiring age if less than 65
1 week's pay	For each complete year of employment in which the employee was not below age 22 but was below age 41
½ week's pay	For each complete year of employment in which the employee was not below age 18 but was below age 22

(when an employee reaches 64, he or she loses one twelfth of the redundancy entitlement for every complete month over this age, until it tapers to zero at 65)

Health authority refund of statutory payments

If a practice is required to make a statutory redundancy payment to an employee for whom they have been receiving direct reimbursements before the date of dismissal, the health authority will refund in part or in whole (as appropriate) the amount paid. Under the new practice staff scheme health authorities have the discretion to determine the percentage of the payment directly reimbursed. Thus, the authority's or board's contribution towards a statutory payment may be uncertain or limited in extent. Increasingly, practices will be responsible for funding a sizable proportion of any payment due.

The right to time off for job hunting

An employee who is given notice because of redundancy is entitled to reasonable time off with pay during working hours to look for another job or arrange training for future employment. Employees are entitled to time off if they have had two years' continuous employment.

Fair and unfair selection for redundancy

As far as possible, objective criteria, precisely defined and capable of being applied in an independent way, should be used when determining who is made redundant. This ensures that employees are not unfairly selected for redundancy. Examples of such criteria include length of service, attendance record, experience and capability. The chosen criteria must be consistently applied by any employer irrespective of the size of his undertaking, and the decision should normally reflect some combination of the above criteria.

The dismissal of an employee selected for redundancy will be automatically unfair if it is for one of the reasons listed in Box 16.2. In addition, dismissal may be considered unfair when the reason is redundancy but the circumstances apply equally to other employees who have not been selected. An employer must be able to show that in selecting an employee for redundancy they have compared the employee, using the agreed objective criteria, with those other employees who might have been made redundant, and that having done so it emerges that the employee was fairly selected. A claim of unfair selection, and thus potentially unfair dismissal, may also arise if the employer has failed to undertake a reasonable search for alternative work throughout the organization.

Box 16.2: Unfair selection for redundancy

- The selection is because of trade union membership (or non-membership) or activity, *or*
- The selection is discriminatory on grounds of race or sex

Selection for voluntary redundancy

It is acceptable for employees to volunteer for redundancy and for the employer to select from among the volunteers those who are to be made redundant. This approach avoids the need for compulsion and has a less demoralizing and disruptive effect on staff. But 'voluntary redundancy' is often more expensive since long service employees will often volunteer and thus attract higher redundancy payments. It is not unusual to offer enhanced redundancy payments as an incentive to attract volunteers. But this voluntary method can leave an imbalance in the skills and experience of the remaining staff. An employer is not obliged to select volunteers for redundancy.

Early retirement can also be a costly method. Whereas voluntary redundancy involves a one-off payment, early retirement often involves a long-term financial commitment in the form of a pension.

Selection for compulsory redundancy

If voluntary redundancy or early retirement does not yield suitable volunteers you then have to consider which criteria to use for compulsory redundancy.

- *Skills or qualifications*. Selection based on these helps to ensure that a balance of skills and qualifications can be retained. It may be appropriate to take account of other aptitudes as well as formal qualifications.
- *'Last in, first out'*. Although this criterion is objective, easy to apply, readily understood and widely accepted, you could lose those employees with key skills.
- *Standard of work performance or aptitude for work*. Ensure that you have objective evidence to support selection on this basis, otherwise you could be faced with a successful claim for unfair dismissal.
- *Attendance or disciplinary records*. Take care to ensure that redundancy selection according to these criteria is based on accurate information. Before selecting on the basis of attendance it is vital to know the reasons for and extent of any absences; this is particularly important when considering sickness absence. An employer should look very carefully at the duration of the spells of sickness, e.g. whether an employee has had one continuous long bout of sickness or whether the absences were of a more intermittent nature but over a longer period.

Applying the selection criteria

In deciding on the selection criteria, the most important consideration for the future viability of the practice is to maintain a balanced workforce after the redundancy has been completed. Specific skills, flexibility, adaptability and an employee's approach to work are likely to be the most relevant considerations for the future success of the practice. In some circumstances senior staff may need to be employed on a lower grade of work and as a consequence may displace and cause a redundancy among more junior staff.

It is not enough, however, to draw up objective criteria to ensure a fair and reasonable selection. The selection will still be unfair if the criteria are carelessly or mistakenly applied.

Consultation

If redundancies are proposed,. consultation with recognized trade unions or elected representatives must start at least 30 days before where more than 20 redundancies are contemplated. Although statute law only prescribes consultation for multiple redundancies, case law shows that individual redundancy requires consultation to be carried out. The law also requires that the consultation is meaningful; it is not only just to inform. For individual redundancies case law indicates that discussion should address the following:

* why and how individuals have been selected
* possible ways of avoiding redundancy
* possible alternative work.

The Government is proposing to remove the 20 employees threshold and is considering a different form of consultation for small numbers of employees.

Advice and assistance

Great care must be exercised if you are considering making any employee redundant, otherwise you may be faced with a claim for compensation for an unfair dismissal. At the earliest opportunity you should contact your local BMA office for expert advice on how to handle this difficult, and fortunately very rare, situation. Far too often redundancy has been used as a pretext for dismissing employees who are not in fact redundant. The consequences of using redundancy for the purpose of dismissing on grounds of inefficiency or incapability, when there is no genuine redundancy, can be very serious indeed. A successful claim of unfair dismissal can involve an employer in paying out a five figure sum as compensation. This compensatory award cannot be offset against taxation, nor can any part of it be reimbursed by the health authority.

Consultation is essential before the final decision to make someone redundant. This allows for ideas and suggestions which could help to avoid the redundancy.

17 NHS pensions for practice staff

Where to obtain advice and assistance

NHS Pensions Agency helpline, Tel: 0800 731 3262, Fax: 01253 774791. Radcliffe Medical Press has recently published *Staff Pensions in General Practice*, John Lindsay and Norman Ellis. This chapter is an amended version of Chapter 1 of this book.

A successful campaign

For many years, GP practice staff themselves, together with GPs and various trade unions and professional associations, have sought to have the NHS pension scheme extended to include practice staff. In 1993, Ministers finally gave approval in principle to this change. However, this decision was subject to further consideration of the cost involved. As the months went by, it became increasingly clear that a further intensive public campaign was needed to ensure that this commitment was implemented.

In May 1996, the British Medical Association launched a campaign to persuade the Government to honour the commitment. In conjunction with the trade union UNISON, it financed a poster and petition campaign, sending publicity material to every practice, highlighting the injustice and asking patients for their support. The campaign was widened to include the Association of Managers in General Practice, the Association of Medical Secretaries, Practice Managers, Administrators and Receptionists, the Association of London Practice Nurses, the Chartered Society of

Physiotherapists, the Community and District Nursing Association, and MSF (including the Health Visitors' Association). The Royal College of Nursing and other staff organizations continued to campaign in their own right. Petitions were delivered to 10 Downing Street and personally to the Chancellor of the Exchequer. The Chairman of the BMA Superannuation Committee, Dr Simon Fradd, met the Secretary of State on several occasions, as well as the Chancellor. Many MPs made representations on behalf of constituents employed in GP practices. Two hundred thousand people signed the petition and petition forms were continuing to flood in when the Secretary of State announced in December 1996 that the Government had decided to open the scheme to practice staff. This belated decision was of course greeted with delight by practice staff throughout the country.

Joining the NHS pension scheme

The NHS pension scheme has been open to GP practice staff from 1 September 1997; since that date all eligible staff have automatically become members of the scheme unless they chose to opt out.

All staff are eligible to join the scheme if they have an employment contract and are involved in providing services to NHS patients. However, eligibility is not restricted to staff who have direct patient contact; it also includes other staff who help to run the practice. Eligible staff include:

- whole-time and part-time staff
- staff from all practices whether fundholding or non-fundholding, single-handed or partnerships
- doctors employed as assistant practitioners, including those in the Doctors' Retainer Scheme
- staff for whom the practice receives no direct reimbursement of staff costs from the health authority
- cleaners, gardeners and other manual staff.

Practice staff cannot join if they are:

- employed by an agency
- involved in private or commercial duties.

Buying additional years of service

Practice staff are able to buy extra years of service, subject to the normal scheme limits. They may also consider other options such as the in-house Equitable Life additional voluntary contribution (AVC) scheme or free-standing additional voluntary contributions (FSAVCs).

Staff who have personal pensions

Because the NHS pension scheme was not available to them in the past, some practice staff have purchased personal pensions (or similar retirement-type policies) or their employers have done so on their behalf. These staff need to give careful consideration to their future pension plans and detailed guidance on this important matter is provided in *Staff Pensions in General Practice* published by Radcliffe Medical Press.

NHS injury benefits scheme

This scheme is entirely separate from the NHS pension scheme. It provides additional benefits to someone who is unable to work as a result of an injury, illness or disease which has been caused by their NHS duties. Unfortunately, this benefit is not available to GP practice staff.

Special class status

Some practice nurses who have previously worked in the NHS may be able to retire at age 55, rather than the normal retirement age of 60.

Administrative arrangements

The NHS pension scheme is administered by the NHS Pensions Agency in England and Wales, the Scottish Office Pensions Agency in Scotland and the Superannuation Branch of the Department of Health and Personal Social Services in Northern Ireland.

The NHS Pensions Agency has distributed to all practices an Employer's Guide which is intended to assist GPs and practice managers to deal with the necessary administrative aspects of the scheme at local level. These include:

- issuing information about the scheme to employees
- obtaining employees' signatures to confirm they have received the information
- ensuring that the opting in or opting out forms have been completed
- the calculation and payment of employee and employer contributions
- completing and forwarding to the Agency the forms needed to administer the scheme
- obtaining further information as necessary via the Helpline.

The Agency has a special Helpline and fax number for GPs and their staff:

Tel: 0800 731 3262
Fax: 01253 774791.

Contributions to the scheme are collected by Hartshead Solway Ltd (*see* Appendix A) which performs this task on behalf of the Agency. Hartshead Solway have established a separate Helpline and fax number to deal with any enquiries about contributions:

Tel: 01142 739992
Fax: 01142 731314.

The NHS Pensions Agency also appointed, by competitive tender, an outside organization to provide training for GP practices in administering the scheme. This is the Benefits Agency Training Operations organization. They have produced a training supplement, in paper and electronic format, which is designed to help practices to carry out the tasks required of the employer, particularly the completion of scheme documentation. Details are available from the Pensions Agency Helpline.

18 The practice staff scheme

Where to obtain advice and assistance

LMCs and health authorities are important sources for advice. BMA members can also contact their local BMA office.

The 1990 changes to the Statement of Fees and Allowances (the Red Book) introduced important changes to the ancillary staff scheme, now known as the practice staff scheme. These include the cash limiting of funds available for reimbursement, health authority discretion to reimburse directly any proportion of staff costs and the removal of all restrictions on both the range and number of practice staff that may attract reimbursement, and on the reimbursement of related staff salaries.

Staff in post on 31 March 1990 were largely protected from the effects of these changes. This protection applies to individual post holders rather than the posts as such. They can be paid reasonable cost of living increases and contractually agreed salary increments without putting at risk their protected status. However, practices have to submit new applications for direct reimbursement for existing staff (including related ancillary staff) if they wish to either:

- increase their hours of employment *or*
- increase the percentage of salary or other costs reimbursed *or*
- increase salary levels (other than reasonable cost of living increases or contractual increments) *or*
- modify substantially their duties, e.g. as a consequence of promotion.

These new applications for existing staff have to be accompanied by a job description specifying the duties and responsibilities of the post, together with an employment contract providing details of arrangements for salary review. Thus, practices should provide comprehensive job descriptions for their existing staff. This will help them to press their case for reimbursement to continue when an existing post holder leaves and they wish to appoint a successor. As has been pointed out in Chapter 3, job descriptions should be separate and distinct from contracts defining the main purpose, main tasks and scope of the job. Because both reasonable salary increases and annual scale increments agreed with staff before 1 April 1990 will be honoured under the transitional arrangements, it is vital that practices ensure that these agreements are made clear in their staff contracts.

New staff

In exercising their discretion in determining whether and at what level to reimburse staff costs, health authorities are required to make decisions according to their plans for developing the service, their cash allocation, the circumstances of individual practices and the need to deal consistently with practices in similar circumstances. Apart from those posts occupied by staff employed before 1 April 1990, and thereby covered by the transitional arrangements described above, all other posts will be reviewed by the health authority at intervals no more frequent than every three years. In these reviews the health authority will be expected to pay particular attention to the benefits of ensuring the continuity of employment of experienced or skilled staff, to give reasonable notice of reviews and to implement changes fairly.

What can be reimbursed?

The total amount that can be reimbursed may include any proportion of the following items:

• salary
• employer's National Insurance contributions
• employer's contributions to the National Health Service superannuation scheme or a qualifying private superannuation scheme
• training costs, including course fees and travel and subsistence expenses
• payment to an agency for staff costs (including salaries, National Insurance and superannuation)

- redundancy payments
- salary for sick leave and maternity leave, net of any compensation due on statutory sick pay and statutory maternity pay and salary for paid holidays and attendance at training courses
- salary of relief staff, including practice staff covering for absent colleagues.

Once a post is approved, reimbursement should normally continue at a similar level, unless on review the health authority finds that there has been a significant change in local circumstances.

How to apply for reimbursement

A practice may apply for the direct reimbursement of costs for both directly employed staff and agency staff. (Agency staff can include health authority staff working in a health centre – apart from attached district nurses, health visitors and midwives – university staff or hospital staff, and staff employed by someone else who shares their services with the practice.) In the case of health authority staff working in a health centre, the practice should agree with the authority duties, hours, minimum qualifications and experience, and itemized charges associated with the post. If the practice is dissatisfied with the proposed charge they can request independent arbitration.

Health authorities determine the proportion and type of payment to be reimbursed, the date from which it will be made, and the minimum qualifications and experience staff may be required to have. These bodies will also review, at intervals no more frequent than three years, approvals or the conditions under which these were given.

When assessing the minimum qualifications and experience that may be required of practice staff, health authorities will take account of the standards adopted by national regulatory bodies or bodies awarded recognized qualifications. In the case of administrative and clerical staff, they will pay particular attention to experience and competence gained through in-service training. (Practice nurses will be expected to hold an appropriate qualification registered or recorded on the Professional Register maintained by the United Kingdom Central Council for Nursing, Midwifery and Health Visiting.)

Practices can, of course, continue to employ staff outside the practice staff scheme. But, if they do so they will not be paid any direct reimbursement. Any costs incurred will be reimbursed through the indirect reimbursement of expenses. Although any staff employed outside the scheme are not subject to the health authority's requirements in respect of qualifications, training and experience, general practitioners' terms of service have been amended to require them to take reasonable care to ensure that any employee is both suitably qualified and competent to discharge their duties.

Appendix A

Local BMA offices and staff

England

Bristol

4th Floor
Centre Gate
Colston Avenue
Bristol BS1 4TR
Tel: 0117 922 7645
Fax: 0117 925 2494

Cambridge

10 Downing Street
Cambridge CB2 3DS
Tel: 01223 364539
Fax: 01223 464743

Exeter

Portland House
Langbrook Street
Exeter EX4 6AB
Tel: 01392 276661

Mersey
(includes Isle of Man)

35 Seymour Terrace
Seymour Street
Liverpool L3 5PE
Tel: 0151 709 5660
Fax: 0151 709 5376

North East

First Floor
Holland Park C
Holland Drive
Fenham Barracks
Newcastle NE2 4LD
Tel: 0191 261 7131
Fax: 0191 261 6203

North Thames	BMA House Tavistock Square London WC1H 9JP Tel: 0171 388 8296 Fax: 0171 383 6911
North West	Bartree House 460 Palatine Road Northenden Manchester M22 4DJ Tel: 0161 945 8989 Fax: 0161 945 5045
Oxford	Cranbrook House 287 Banbury Road Summertown Oxford OX2 7JF Tel: 01865 559621 Fax: 01865 558082
South Thames	Venture House 15 High Street Purley Surrey CR8 2XA Tel: 0181 660 5558 Fax: 0181 668 0117
Trent	301 Glossop Road Sheffield S10 2HL Tel: 0114 272 1705 Fax: 0114 275 1686
West Midlands	36 Harborne Road Edgbaston Birmingham B15 3AJ Tel: 0121 456 1402 Fax: 0121 456 3439
Winchester (includes Channel Islands)	Star Lane House Staple Gardens Winchester SO23 8SR Tel: 01962 856760 Fax: 01962 856761

Yorkshire

Gladstone House
Redvers Close
Lawnswood Business Park
Leeds LS16 6SS
Tel: 0113 230 4417
Fax: 0113 230 6144

Scotland

South East Scotland

3 Hill Place
Edinburgh EH8 9EQ
Tel: 0131 662 4820
Fax: 0131 667 6933

West of Scotland

2 Woodside Place
Glasgow G3 7QF
Tel: 0141 332 1862
Fax: 0141 332 2259

North of Scotland

56 Queen's Street
Aberdeen AB1 6YE
Tel: 01224 323311
Fax: 01224 322723

Wales

1 Cleeve House
Cardiff Business Park
Llanishen
Cardiff CF4 5GJ
Tel: 01222 766277
Fax: 01222 766162

Northern Ireland

61 Malone Road
Belfast BT9 6SA
Tel: 01232 663272
Fax: 01232 666318

BMA Professional Services Ltd

London	BMA House Tavistock Square London WC1H 9JP Tel: 0171 383 6743 Fax: 0171 383 6813
South Thames	Croudace House 97 Godstone Road Caterham Surrey CR3 6XQ Tel: 01883 331215 Fax: 01883 331216
North Thames	York House Empire Way Wembley Middlesex HA9 0PA Tel: 0181 900 0444 Fax: 0181 903 6185
Trent	Rodney House Castle Gate Nottingham NG1 7AW Tel: 0115 948 0788 * Fax: 0115 948 0787
North West	Warrant House High Street Altrincham Cheshire WA14 1PZ Tel: 0161 928 7704 Fax: 0161 928 7723

BMA Services Ltd

Aberdeen	56 Queens Road Aberdeen AB15 4YE Tel: 01224 323311
Belfast	Second and Third Floor 102 Lisburn Road Belfast BT9 6AG Tel: 01232 664609
Birmingham	Maybrook House Queensway Halesowen Birmingham B63 4AH Tel: 0121 585 6474
Bristol	25 Osprey Court Hawkfield Business Park Whitchurch Bristol BS14 0BB Tel: 0117 964 0777
Cardiff	Unit 15 Lambourne Crescent Cardiff Business Park Cardiff CF4 5GG Tel: 01222 766988
Dartford	Instone House Instone Road Dartford Kent DA1 2AG Tel: 01322 272270
Edinburgh	Stanhope House 12 Stanhope Place Edinburgh EH12 5HH Tel: 0131 313 0210

Exeter	Third Floor Portland House Longbrook Street Exeter EX4 6AB Tel: 01392 422456
Glasgow	Breckenridge House 274 Sauchiehall Street Glasgow G2 3EH Tel: 0141 332 1862
Leeds	Gladstone House Redvers Close Lawnswood Business Park Leeds LS16 6UU Tel: 0113 230 6100
Leicester	Premier House 29 Rutland Street Leicester LE1 1RE Tel: 0116 265 0354
Liverpool	35 Seymour Terrace Seymour Street Liverpool L3 5PE Tel: 0151 709 3599
Manchester	Bartree House 460 Palatine Road Northenden Manchester M22 4DJ Tel: 0161 945 5445
Newcastle	Holland Park C Holland Drive Fenham Barracks Newcastle NE2 4LD Tel: 0191 261 9661

Nottingham

Huntingdon House
278–280 Huntingdon Street
Nottingham NG1 3LY
Tel: 0115 952 4333

Sheffield

305 Glossop Road
Sheffield S10 2HL
Tel: 0114 279 7813

Uxbridge

3 The Grand Union Office Park
Packet Boat Lane
Uxbridge
Middlesex UB8 2GH
Tel: 01895 850350

North London

Bartholomew Court
60–61 High Street
Waltham Cross
Herts EN8 7DD
Tel: 01992 638121

For general insurance enquiries, the Free Quoteline number is 0500 181 099. This office is based at Colchester.

# Appendix B

Advisory, Conciliation and Arbitration Service (ACAS)
Brandon House
180 Borough High Street
London SE1 1LW
Tel: 0171 210 3613

Association of Managers in General Practice (AMGP)
Suite 308
The Foundry
156 Blackfriars Road
London SE1 8EN
Tel: 0171 721 7080

Association of Medical Secretaries, Practice Managers, Administrators and Receptionists (AMSPAR)
Tavistock House North
Tavistock Square
London WC1H 9LN
Tel: 0171 387 6005

British Medical Association
BMA House
Tavistock Square
London WC1H 9JP
Tel: 0171 387 4499

Department for Education and Employment
Sanctuary Buildings
Great Smith Street
London SW1P 3BT
Tel: 0171 925 5000

GP Forum
92 Baslow Road
Totley
Sheffield S17 4DQ
Tel: 0114 235 1660

Health and Safety Executive (HSE)
Information Centre
Broad Lane
Sheffield S3 7HQ
Tel: 0541 545500

Radcliffe Medical Press Ltd (for PRP course)
18 Marcham Road
Abingdon
Oxon OX14 1AA
Tel: 01235 528820

Royal College of General Practitioners (RCGP)
14 Princes Gate
Hyde Park
London SW7 1PU
Tel: 0171 581 3232
Fax: 0171 225 3046

Royal College of Nursing (RCN)
20 Cavendish Square
London W1M 9AE
Tel: 0171 409 3333

Index